ENTERED JAN 2 7 1997

Fullness of Dissonance

Fullness of Dissonance

Modern Fiction and
the Aesthetics of Music

Daniel C. Melnick

Rutherford • Madison • Teaneck
Fairleigh Dickinson University Press
London and Toronto: Associated University Presses

© 1994 by Associated University Presses, Inc.

All rights reserved. Authorization to photocopy items for internal or personal use, or the internal or personal use of specific clients, is granted by the copyright owner, provided that a base fee of $10.00, plus eight cents per page, per copy is paid directly to the Copyright Clearance Center, 222 Rosewood Drive, Danvers, Massachusetts 01923. [0-8386-3525-3/94 $10.00 + 8¢ pp, pc.]

Associated University Presses
440 Forsgate Drive
Cranbury, NJ 08512

Associated University Presses
25 Sicilian Avenue
London WC1A 2QH, England

Associated University Presses
P.O. Box 338, Port Credit
Mississauga, Ontario
L5G 4L8 Canada

The paper used in this publication meets the requirements
of the American National Standard for Permanence of Paper
for Printed Library Materials Z39.48–1984.

Library of Congress Cataloging-in-Publication Data

Melnick, Daniel C., 1943–
    Fullness of dissonance: modern fiction and the aesthetics of
music / Daniel C. Melnick.
       p.   cm.
    Includes bibliographical references and index.
    ISBN 0-8386-3525-3
    1. Fiction—19th century—History and criticism. 2. Fiction—
20th century—History and criticism. 3. Music and literature. 4.
Music—and the aesthetics of music.
PN3499.M45 1994
809.3'9357—dc20   93-8332

809.39357 M527f

Melnick, Daniel C., 1943–

Fullness of dissonance

PRINTED IN THE UNITED STATES OF AMERICA

Contents

Acknowledgments — vii

1. A Sinister Resonance: Dissonance and the Theory of Modern Fiction — 3
2. Early Romantic Ideas of Music: Rousseau and Beethoven — 16
3. Literature and Music in the Nineteenth Century: From Schopenhauer to Wagner — 29
4. Music and the Modern Imagination: Nietzsche and Schoenberg — 44
5. The Dissonant Aesthetic in Continental Fiction: Proust, Music, and the Reader — 59
6. The Ethic of Dissonance: A Study of Mann's *Doctor Faustus* — 79
7. Music and Modern British Fiction: Dissonant *Ulysses*— A Study of How to Read Joyce — 101
8. Conclusion: On the Discoveries of Dissonance in Modern Fiction — 126

Notes — 135
Bibliography — 149
Index — 157

Acknowledgments

The writing of *Fullness of Dissonance* was generously supported by a National Endowment for the Humanities Fellowship, by an NEH grant to study at a "Literature and the Other Arts" Summer Seminar led by Robert M. Adams, as well as by a Cleveland State University Research and Creative Activities Grant. Parts of the chapters on Joyce and Proust appeared in earlier incarnations in *Twentieth Century Literature* and *Modern Language Quarterly*, respectively. An early version of a dozen pages particularly in chapters 1 and 3 appeared in *Modern Fiction Studies*. A few paragraphs of the discussion of Conrad were published in another version as part of an essay on Conrad in *The Missouri Review*, subsequently reprinted in *Modern Critical Views: Joseph Conrad*, edited by Harold Bloom.

I am grateful for the encouragement, criticism, and support offered by friends, colleagues, and students at Cleveland State University and elsewhere; especially by Matt Hazelrig, Ronald Manuto, and Timothy Steyskal, each of whom read and thoughtfully commented on parts of the manuscript at various stages; also, in the beginning by Thomas Flanagan, Robert Tracy, and the late Mark Schorer; and particularly by my brother David Melnick and my wife, Jeanette Arax Melnick, whose painting of Joyce, Mann, Proust, and Schoenberg appears on the jacket. This book is dedicated to the memory of my parents, Esther Altabe Melnick and Perry Julius Melnick.

Fullness of Dissonance

1
A Sinister Resonance: Dissonance and the Theory of Modern Fiction

I

Discussions of modern literature's ties to music are to be found frequently in essays, reviews, and in several books, but from Walter Pater to Roland Barthes, the paragraphs of memorable speculation and even the full analyses seem often to lead to few sustained conclusions, to be spectacularly abortive or oddly ornamental. With some significant exceptions, critical inquiry seems to become the occasion for displays of civilized culture or, at times, of apocalyptic critical speculation.

One thinks of the typical and nicely provocative remarks in Geoffrey Hartman's *Criticism in the Wilderness*. The Romantic (and modernist) "image" is, he writes, "a resonance, a musical as well as a visual phenomenon." He laments the lack of a vocabulary with which to address the matter, and suggests that "poetics has barely begun to struggle with this issue, to take back its own from music." He asks: "Is there such difference between writing and music? . . . Or is music not representation which has broken with representation, and that *like all art* is carried by the 'passion' of that . . . breaking" to yield a form of art based in "indeterminacy?"[1] Music can indeed be understood as a form of writing which has broken with the representational function of words, and Hartman's remarks have in their background the post-Renaissance anxiety that both literature and particularly the ideal of a musicalized art will not be able to overcome the break between transcendent imagination and experience. Hartman is allowing the hope that such musical form offers an access to freedom, an indeterminacy, which liberates us from the prison of a broken time, a fallen epoch. Yet his speculations are brief, and their fleet brilliance consciously withholds the vocabulary and conception for a sustained exploration of music's tie to modern literature.

Why do discussions of this subject tend to evanesce into unsatisfying speculation? On the one hand, this effect may stem from a concern about the terms of the critical discussion of music, for they can seem ungrounded—promising, and even spectacular, yet finally a quicksilver patina, knowing and unsatisfactory. On the other hand, the evanescence of such speculations may also be the reflexive effect of discussing an art which calls attention to its own insubstantiality, its lack of representation, and so which calls into question the substance and reference of any intellectual (or other) construct attempting to pin down its significance. But the reason for this difficulty is not only such concern about the art which so easily turns back upon itself to obscure and invalidate its own description.

The unsatisfying nature of speculation about music and modern literature also stems, I think, from a fundamental, historical premise of the commentaries over the past century or so. Such discussions—either brief or full-fledged—make certain assumptions that appear suspect in our time of exacerbated self-consciousness about the nature of art and of critical discourse itself. And so many commentators on literature and music mute or cut short their point, as if they had touched on something dubious, perverse, and—the Conradian word, again—evanescent. It is an assumed attitude about the "aesthetic" which quickly and finally atomizes such commentaries, for the aestheticism implied is—for the most part—discredited today, a throwback to the late nineteenth century before all the arts seemed fully to throw off the shackles of earlier convention and rush into the modern. The musicalization of poetry and fiction can seem almost fatally associated with the dubious, incompletely liberated premodern aestheticist attempt to create a sensuous and self-sustaining Paterian "beauty" in literature which abjures even as it is entrammeled by bourgeois reality.

Yet this discrediting suspicion suggests a lack of understanding about the actual nature of the connection between music and modern literature. When Conrad and Mann, Eliot and Rilke, Woolf and Lawrence, Proust and Joyce assert the tie between music and their works, they are concerned not merely with the apparent sensuous aestheticism that partly beguiled them as youthful writers. Rather, the mature practitioners of the modern present a view of music which belongs to a deeper and longer-lived tradition than aestheticism. The flow of ideas about music from the Romantics to the Symbolists and to Nietzsche constitutes a crucial, revelatory source of modernism; and for twentieth-century European aesthetics, it has been the focus of brilliant illumination on the part of Adorno, Bloch, Barthes, and others. There is a need—as George Steiner has well argued in *Language and Silence*—to integrate that tradition of thought about music into the parlance and practice of critical work, particularly on the major modernist novelists in English.[2] That tradition offers the basis and occasion of a sustained analysis as well as the profoundly rewarding pleasure of exploring how two arts in a given cultural period mesh and nurture one another. What René Welleck called for at mid-century is still a valid prescription: to analyze "the genuine parallelisms" in thinking about music and literature as they arise "from identical or similar social or intellectual backgrounds."[3]

An initial example from the work of Joseph Conrad—the cautiously masked, self-critical cosmopolite among early modern novelists in English—will help me to begin formulating the significance of the nineteenth-century European intellectual background for novelists in the twentieth century. In that background and tradition from the Romantic period to the fin de siècle, the linkage of music to literature proclaims a potent, shaping aesthetic which is embedded in the modern imagination and is central to its theory. A brief look at *Heart of Darkness* will indicate the significance of the link I want to explore. In his prefacing remarks to the novella, Conrad asserts a musical analogy at that crucial point in his comments when he comes closest to suggesting the significance of his novella. Up to this point in the Author's Note, he has noted that the work presents "experience pushed a little (and only very little) beyond the actual facts of the case for the perfectly legitimate, I believe, purpose of bringing it home to the mind and bosom of the reader."[4] A bit coyly here, in light of the work's subversions, Conrad suggests a tie between the reader, the text, and experience, a tie which is intentionally paradoxical and disturbing: "to bring home," as he says, the "experience" of the "heart of darkness." Conrad then presents a musical analogy which—as Mark Schorer early noted[5]—"anticipated" what the modernist musicalization of fiction signifies by using that analogy as a means to define the hoped-for potency of Conrad's symbolic, ambiguous art:

> It was like another art altogether. That sombre theme had to be given a sinister resonance, a tonality of its own, a continued vibration that I hoped would hang in the air and dwell on the ear after the last note had been struck.[6]

Conrad's analogy suggests three features of musicalized fiction. First, there is its subversion of the reader's complacent or conventional impression of experience, its "sinister resonance"; second, there is its fictive declaration of a "tonality of its own," self-sustained, separate from that of the conventional, harmoniously accessible imagination; and third, there is its continued open-ended impact or "vibration" entering into and activating its extraordinary imaginative activity in the reader—its resonance "brought home" as he wrote, "to dwell on the ear." This passage, using the metaphor of music in the midst of the shoptalk of the Author's Note, is Conrad's means momentarily to create a microcosm of his art and its hoped-for effect. Suspended for a moment here is the seeming substantiality of his matter-of-fact prefacing note, with its voice of the author as practitioner, and in its place he offers the instability and thrilling insubstantiality of analogy, a brief projection and reminder of the qualities of the fiction itself. The musical analogy is the crucial means Conrad finds here for announcing and prefiguring the actual aim of his novel.

The passage has moved beyond the aestheticist rhetoric which celebrates and embodies the sensuously "beautiful" and symbol-laden Paterian moment—that is to say, beyond the aesthete's essentially still-born yearning for a renaissance of elaborate and beautiful anti-bourgeois art (and life). Certainly, for example in his Preface to *The Nigger of the "Narcissus,"* Conrad establishes a seemingly Paterian goal for his fiction, the ideal of bringing to bear the "magic suggestiveness of music" as a means of reviving the "worn" and deadened language of narrative, finally in order "to make you see, . . . that glimpse of truth for which you have forgotten to ask."[7] Conrad's rhetoric does initially employ the "aestheticist" motif of calling into question the deadened language and complacent substantiality of ordinary bourgeois experience and perception, but he does not replace it with an exquisitely contrived sensibility. Indeed, when Conrad projects the "sinister resonance" of *Heart of Darkness*, the most striking implication of his image and strategy concerns the admission of the inharmonious, the assaulting darkness, into the complex relations Conrad's work develops between the reader, the text, and experience. Dissonance—and not a conventionally beautiful harmony—is the new form, the embedded metaphor and philosophic aim in which Conrad's prefatory remarks find their roots.

A brief reconnaissance of *Heart of Darkness* itself clarifies the nature of the analogy—of fiction as a sinister resonance, as a dissonance. The text asserts itself, it is often noted, as a clash of "voices" in which the truth or clarity of any one voice becomes suspect. For example, Kurtz's voice, Marlow says, has "the gift of expression, the bewildering, the illuminating, the most exalted and the most contemptible, the pulsating stream of light, or the deceitful flow from the heart of an impenetrable darkness."[8] Such are the conflicted paradoxes into which Marlow's own narrative voice is driven; at times it is driven even into silence, and at such points the framing narrator stumbles back in. As each voice Marlow hears disintegrates and disappears, a new voice takes up and reechoes in a continual process of activation and exhaustion and reactivation. Such is the plan of the novel and the paradigm of Conrad's imagination, a paradigm and a process that Conrad wishes to carry over into the reader's consciousness. A part of the reader's task is to suspend or re-see the entire gilded, conventional world with its imperial burden of bourgeois materialism and idealism, as if that world of experience were infused with and created within the imagination. Only now, in the reader's vantage, can that world's actual flickerings and darknesses of spirit be perceived. This plan is evident even in Conrad's preface—ever polite and reined-in—as it hints at the dangerous process into which the reader at home in his chair can enter as he reads *Heart of Darkness*. The self-disintegrating voices of the text challenge the reader to suspend the narrator's limitations of anxiety or idealism, to engage the ever unfinished work of insight and critical judgment, and to take up the creative, open-ended, and—in the novelist's view—heroic task of the imaginative process in his or her own consciousness. Dissonance—Conrad's reechoing "sinister resonance"—is a key metaphor for that process.

II

Musical dissonance is a structure of tones unresolved into the familiar cadences of harmonic closure. Dissonance gives form to a declaration of ongoing process and tension, to the refusal to resolve, to the denial of the sense of conventional ending in harmony. As the history of music unfolds in the late nineteenth century, dissonance's declaration of tension and ongoing process becomes increasingly essential to the language of music, and ceases being merely one among many expressive enriching devices for music, as was the case in the Classical period. In the early twentieth century, dissonance becomes the single most effective "language" music can speak in a century of disequilibrium like the one now ending. When modern novelists undertake the musicalization of fiction, their efforts lead not to the writing of harmonious, self-consciously beautiful "musical" prose, but rather to the use of a series of experimental, destabilizing strategies, which, under the guise of musicalization, assume and achieve the effect of dissonance in the novel.

For Joyce, Mann, Proust, Conrad, Gide, or Woolf, musicalizing strategies include the temporal play with the suspension and dislocation of time, the experimental interplay and clashes in voice and style, and the ambiguous layering and fragmenting of narration itself. Given the array of these and other musicalizing strategies, dissonance as a term accrues multiple and shifting meanings, and its tendency is to emphasize the modern text's disordering of earlier novelistic conventions of time, narration, and style. Inevitably, the concept of dissonance in modern fiction grows and shifts as the focus of analysis moves from the practice of one novelist to that of another. In this sense, dissonance—as an analogy and aesthetic perspective—partakes of the richness, variety, and suggestiveness of symbol, of a multifaceted symbolic critical construct like the concept of modernism itself.

The definition of dissonance in fiction is further complicated because modern novelists employ musicalizing strategies above all in order to achieve a significant and distinct effect on the reader, an impact which is best understood in terms of the ethical "resonance" of dissonant form. As Conrad suggests in regard to the "sinister resonance" of *Heart of Darkness*, the modern novelist's musicalization of fiction has a profound ethical goal as well as a structural and stylistic one. The impact on the reader which is sought in dissonant narrative is that its experimental destabilization of form will activate the reader's capacity for freed, independent consciousness and judgment. This goal and impact are defined by the seminal ideas about music developed later in the twentieth century by two critical thinkers, Theodor Adorno and Ernst Bloch.

Dissonance, in Adorno's conception, constitutes a key modernist strategy designed to oppose and overcome what he calls "the deceptive moment" in the reception of conventional art: the moment in which the "self-limited" audience is made to feel "in accord with all, accepted and reconciled by all," a moment designed falsely and uncritically to seem "to fulfill men in themselves, to train them for consent" within the order of modern society.[9] The destabilizing form of dissonant art proposes an alternative to such falsifying passivity of reception, an alternative based in radical doubt about the ordinary habits of aesthetic perception. "Dissonances," writes Adorno, "arose as the expressions of tension, contradiction and pain . . . . [T]hey become characters of objective protest" stirring in the reader a searching and creative practice of critical scrutiny,[10]—a consciousness the stirring of which is the goal Conrad avowed, as we saw.

For Adorno, dissonance's "negativity is true to utopia."[11] Dissonant form provides one of the crucial "perspectives"—aesthetic, philosophical, or social—which, Adorno writes in the powerful, exposed conclusion to *Minima Moralia*, "displace and estrange the world, reveal it to be, with its rifts and crevices, as indigent and distorted as it will appear one day in the messianic light."[12] Here Adorno's conception mirrors Ernst Bloch's, even if arising from the former's more bracing critical orientation. Both writers assume that in the dynamic joining of utopian yearning with critical negativity—the sense of the modern century as a century of death—there is a continual and inevitable interaction between utopian and critical perceptions.[13] That dynamic interaction or perspective, Bloch posits in his *Philosophy of Music*, is achieved above all in the experience of the "visionary hearer."[14] The self-scrutiny and divination, which constitute this challenged capacity in us, enable the hearer "to discern the utopian ground of the soul drawing closer."[15] In a century marked by total war and totalizing, technocratic social organization, it is an apocalyptic landscape which Bloch's aesthetic confronts: "As soon as all falls silent on Earth, . . . music will articulate features of the other world, deriving from a different larynx and logos."[16] Bloch presents such hearing as a new "dawn" over a vista of "death and decay," and his conception mixes apocalyptic despair and hope, "a clairvoyance . . . radiating into the void before us."[17] Dissonance, I follow Adorno in arguing, is one of the forms of such perception.

The vision shared by Bloch and Adorno is forecast near the turn of the century by Conrad himself, in his sense of the "sinister resonance" of modern narrative, and likewise in his essay "Henry James: An Appreciation" (with its Paterian echo and retrieval):

> When the last aqueduct shall have crumbled to pieces, the last airship fallen to the ground, the last blade of grass have died upon a dying earth, man, indomitable by his training in resistance to misery and pain, shall set this undiminished light of his eyes against the feeble glow of the sun.[18]

In a synaesthesia of seeing and hearing—of a visionary hearing prefiguring Bloch's insight—"the artistic faculty," Conrad writes, "may find its voice" among one of these last witnesses to the progressive silencing which is equally "like death." Such a voice will confront and test "the heroism of the hearers." And what will be heard in the dissonant pain and irony, the "stoic" and "sardonic" utterances, of that voice by the final group "clustered . . . to watch the last flicker of light on a black sky, to hear the last word uttered in the stilled workshop of the earth?" This voice on the edge of silence, witnessing the end of Western consciousness and emanating from the heart of its darkness, will—Conrad speculates—"formulate, strange as it may appear, some hope now to us utterly inconceivable."[19]

The effect and goal for the novel, which Conrad is evoking, constitute the aim and impact of dissonance in modern narrative. In this critical analogy and aesthetic located in the modern novel, reading is a process that achieves "a constant anticipatory awareness of what is lacking in the present"—in Chris Norris's phrasing of the aesthetic tenet which Bloch shares with Adorno and with deconstruction in its more "utopian" guise.[20] "Art's irreconcilability" to the present moment, writes Peter Osborne about this shared aesthetic, is maintained by having such irreconcilability "consciously introduced into the work . . . as a constructive principle, that is, as a dissonance."[21] Dissonance is, then, the form narrative achieves when modern novelists undertake to musicalize fiction. It is, to alter Pater, the condition to which modern narrative aspires. Its yearning for a transcendence absent here and now is tragically parodied by Mann, and its promise of a fictive, healing play and abundance is comically affirmed by Joyce. An encompassing, dissonant structure of "irreconcilability"—this complex sense of simultaneous potentiality and negation, promise and absence—is to be perceived in each page of modern narrative.

The conception of the modern novel as a "fullness of dissonance" develops from roots deep in nineteenth-century thought. In the following two chapters, I trace that development from Romanticism to Wagner and the Symbolists. The fourth chapter examines the Nietzschean vision of music, which is a crucial source of ideas and insights about dissonance in modern art, in Schoenberg's music as in the modern novel. Subsequent chapters explore how the conception of dissonance illuminates the aim and impact of Proust's *Remembrance of Things Past*, Mann's *Doctor Faustus*, and Joyce's *Ulysses*.

It is above all Nietzsche's idea of Dionysian dissonance which, we shall see, provides an essential perspective exposing the nature of modern, musicalized narrative form, above all its joining of potentiality and negation, of imaginative and critical perception, which two generations later Adorno and Bloch discern at the center of modernism's purpose. In *Ecce Homo*, Nietzsche describes that key, paradoxical joining, as he discusses the formulation of this concept in his first book, *The Birth of Tragedy from the Spirit of Music*. Dionysian dissonance is the aesthetic projection of "*becoming* along with a radical repudiation of the very concept of being."[22] This antinomy is what Claude Lévesque calls "the double step" of dissonance for Nietzsche and the modernists who follow him, a "double step" that repudiates present time and identity even as it continually proposes new, unfolding possibilities of time and identity; it is indeed a double step of anguish and joy.[23] The searching, destabilizing form of Dionysian dissonance in narrative, finally, underlies the Nietzschean concept often noted by critics of modern fiction: "to become what one is, one must not have the faintest notion what one is"[24]—cited for example by Philip Weinstein, John Foster, and others with regard to Lawrence.[25] This implicit ethic of becoming, essential to the idea of dissonance in modern fiction, is also linked to Maurice Blanchot's revelation of how silence and song and the agony of listening cluster together in modernity,[26] and to George Steiner's analysis of how modern writers seek to bring their language to "the threshold of that condition" of music's "deeper, more numinous . . . energy" and beyond toward silence itself.[27] As well, the aesthetic and ethic of dissonance are linked to Ihab Hassan's exploration of how Orpheus enacts his fate particularly in our century's fictions.[28]

III

Much Anglo-American criticism of music's tie to the modern novel has heretofore favored an emphasis and approach based on other, quite different theoretical assumptions. Music is usually seen as an aspect of the techniques by which modern novelists structure their works (as Calvin Brown shows in his studies),[29] by which the chaos of inner association and outer dissociation in the twentieth century can be tamed or at least given a controlling form—either through the imitation of musical effects (as Ezra Pound early noted about *Ulysses*)[30] or through the yearning of characters for musical transcendence (this is one of Alex Aronson's key concerns, for example, in *Music and the Novel*[31]). Such emphases on a missing or imposed form, a yearned-for harmony, develop from one of several modernist "traditions," this one stressing the invocation of music as a means of achieving order over chaos, of establishing control over structure, theme, or the juxtaposition of materials. This formalist tradition shapes the usual critical approach to my subject; its assumptions are at the root of certain brilliant technical experiments in fiction and provide the occasion for the modernist assertion (from Yeats, Eliot, and the "Pound tradition") of the musicalized formal image as avatar and symbol of a transcendent, autonomous, aristocratic, ideal art in which sense and spirit are an identity. Yet there is another lineage of modernism that my analysis assumes, one which employs a musical aesthetic to define and confirm the open-ended, exploratory, freed, and creative aesthetic state celebrated from proto-modernists like Rousseau, Baudelaire, and Nietzsche, onward. This is the tradition out of which the discussions of dissonance I cite partly emerge, and it is clear in them that these two traditions of autonomous form and imaginative liberation are intertwined. As Carl Dahlhaus comments in *Schoenberg and the New Music*, a musical art can "represent an element of freedom precisely because it is autonomous."[32]

The two modernist traditions—valuing autonomous, formal order or ontological critical freedom—at their best interpenetrate each

Dissonance and the Theory of Modern Fiction

other. A dissonant aesthetic illuminates this mutual enrichment, which is, of course, also explored in other approaches to modernist theory, for example, in the feminist understanding of the dancing body's role in modernism (see Françoise Meltzer's study[33]). My focus is on how the autonomous musicalized forms in modernist narratives inevitably incorporate—as dissonances—the unstable, the partial and ambiguous, the multiple and provisional possibilities inherent in the disorder of the actual. The symbols of illumination and darkness in Conrad, for example, proclaim no eternal, idealized order, but rather establish a dissonant continuum of contradictory meanings that assault the reader as they give one access to freedom of perception. In the dissonant fictions I will be exploring, images of experience are transformed in the reader's consciousness into images of fictive becoming; experience is "pushed beyond" actuality in order to engage the reader in an exploration that puts into question the conventional orderings of perception and opens him or her to a freed imaginative process. That spurred, fictive re-seeing is what is meant by the fictive becoming achieved by dissonant form.

Yet one might further ask why critic and novelist would want to turn to the metaphor of music and the idea of dissonance in order to bear the weight of these aesthetic and ethical perceptions. It could well be argued that Shakespeare's richly ambiguous language or Emily Brontë's narrative complexity accomplish rather parallel purposes, and they confront the reader without encumbering the process of understanding them with such a construct. This seems true, at least of Brontë, yet the notion of a musicalized literature is a self-conscious element and source of creative ferment occupying the imagination of modern writers to a degree beyond even the Renaissance interest in the link between poetry and musica humana, a link expressed also in the "untuning of the skies" which is Dryden's and Handel's musical emblem for the apocalyptic triumph of Christ over their savage present.

Earlier writers, of course, intensively used techniques of formal dislocation without recourse to a musical aesthetic; one thinks of certain works by Swift, Sterne, Blake, and even Carlyle which distort, defamiliarize, satirize, or alienate in order to attack the defunct, entrappingly habitual order of consciousness in their societies. Yet a pivotal difference between the modernists and these often lacerated oppositionists, one which a dissonant aesthetic enables us to pinpoint, is that modern novelists present the disjunctions and negations in their vision as the very source of meaning, as the only possible positing of the form of freedom in a time when the meaningful has collapsed into silence. Musical dissonance shapes and embodies this modern sense of the uses of silence and disjunction. Ihab Hassan's related insights into the role of silence in the Orphic song of modern texts focus on writers other than the modernists I study whose dissonant practice and ambition are world-encompassing, whereas Hassan takes up writers who practice on the avant-garde edge where all compass tends to vanish into silence.

The concern in modernism with discord itself as an image and spur for a freed, searching, and fertile imagination stems most apparently from the milieu of the late Romantic period. Above all, the ambition of Wagner's operas to create a synaesthetic artwork of the future was a mesmerizing force, and in Paris and Vienna composers were creating revolutionary scores in response particularly to the liberation of Wagnerian chromaticism, with its subversion of traditional harmonic practice; one thinks of Mahler and Debussy and then Schoenberg. There are extraordinary parallels which were formulated across the arts in this period. Kandinsky wrote to Schoenberg at the beginning of their friendship:

> I am certain that our own modern harmony is not to be found in the 'geometric' way, but rather in the antigeometric, antilogical way. And this way is that of 'dissonances in *art*,' in painting, therefore just as much as in music.[34]

Commentators like Carl Schorske and Frederick Karl have noted the many overt links—this between Schoenberg and Kandinsky, or for another example, that between Wagner and the Symbolists and Surrealists.[35] There is a fullness of dissonance across the modern arts, a series of linked "secret languages," in Robert Morgan's phrase.[36]

Finally, however, it is not in the immediate stimulus and background of musical culture that the fullest reason for the modern writer's fascination with music is to be found. Rather, it is to be located in the place that music had gradually come to assume in the Western imagination over the hundred and fifty years preceding the outbreak of the first World War. Modern novelists create texts which would join with music "almost alone in bearing the burden of providing an alternative to the realities of the world" the modernists inherit, as Carl Dahlhaus suggests in *Between Romanticism and Modernism*.[37] Erich Heller in *The Disinherited Mind* gives eloquent voice to this tradition of thinking about music:

> After the seventeenth century, Europe no longer dwelt or worshipped or ruled in buildings created in the image of authentic spiritual vision. For all that was real was an encumbrance to the spirit who, in his turn, only occasionally called on the real, and even then with the embarrassment of an uninvited guest. He was most at home where there was least 'reality'—in music. The music of modern Europe is the one and only art in which it surpassed the achievement of former ages. This is no accident of history: it is the speechless triumph of the spirit in a world of words without deeds and deeds without words.[38]

That formulation of music's import suggests, of course, the turbulence of Romantic vision. The legacy of turbulence besetting nineteenth- and early twentieth-century art (one thinks of the young Joyce or early Yeats and indeed the apprenticeship of most of the modernist writers) profoundly conditioned modern novelists' understanding not only of the musical analogy for fiction, but of the wellsprings of their art.

2
Early Romantic Ideas of Music: Rousseau and Beethoven

I

One of the key contributions of Romanticism to twentieth-century culture is apparent in the significance—for modern literature—of music as it is envisioned by the Romantics, by Rousseau before them, and above all in Beethoven. The Romantic idea of music serves as a metaphor for sensations of inwardness, which, to the philosophers and artists of the time, seemed to loom with increasingly urgent value in human life and simultaneously to be threatened by the actual conditions of existence. For the early Romantic German thinkers—above all Schlegel, Schelling, and Hölderin—music is the language of feeling, the model form for all the arts that comes closest to revealing the inner, emotional "spirit" of man—"ut musica poesis."[1] This art was also seen as a signal participant in the embattled struggle toward the merging of the soul and outer experience in a sought-for humanistic order. In *Faust*, for example, Goethe depicts this struggling, led on by choruses of spirits from first to last scene, toward the imaginative domain in which the All sings, in which the inner appears to infuse and transfigure the outer; yet this desired, symbolic mission itself embodies and is embedded in a partly ironic spectacle of endless striving. Goethe's ideal is that the Faustian striving and the transfiguring music of nature should become one, an identity and metonymy ("as all sing so the All sings!").[2] Yet this metonymy retains the joyous lightness of metaphor, of the fictive, the uselessness (for an atomized, technologized future) that Nietzsche identifies with Goethe's greatness: "Such a spirit," he writes in *Twilight of the*

Idols, "who has become free stands amid the cosmos with a joyous and trusting fatalism, in the faith that only the particular is loathsome, and that all is redeemed and affirmed in the whole—he does not negate any more. Such a faith, however, is the highest of all possible faiths. I have baptized it with the name Dionysus."[3]

Goethe is always sensitive, however, to the cost of the "Dionysian," a cost that becomes part of self-creation and the wholeness itself in which "the All sings." In *Faust* and elsewhere, he dramatizes the risk of failure in striving to bond visionary self and communal other, indeed the risk in the endless process of that struggle. The tragic disconnection between inner and outer, between a world of transcendent beauty and a death to the ordinary living world, marks as well the Erlking and his beautiful daughters singing the alarmed child to his sleep of death before his father's adult obtuseness in Goethe's poem (and Schubert's embodiment in his brilliant and disturbing early song). When other Romantics take up the metaphor of music, they attempt to draw us in to this glorious and costly ideal of a musical transcendence—not so much by persuading us of the transcendental possibility of wholeness, but by evoking for us the paradoxical and contingent struggle toward such transcendence. Such a conception certainly governs Coleridge's practice, for example, in "The Eolian Harp" and in "Kubla Khan," where the mediation of the music of the "damsel with a dulcimer" is invoked so that, finally:

> To such a deep delight would win me
> That with music loud and long,
> I would build that dome in air,
> That sunny dome! Those caves of ice!

Similarly, Keats's "Ode to a Nightingale" presents the experience of listening to and creating music as they are made disturbingly to interact, risking—as both do—a merging with death, a transcendent sensation that would end ordinary existence, and compel—in Coleridge's phrase—all who heard to cry "Beware! Beware!" Yet the paradox and risk in the Ode are transformed by its climax into an affirmation, a celebration of the power of the nightingale's song; its palpable music is linked to an impalpable, transcendent realm, blindness to transfiguring insight, the menaced moment of listening to mute eternity. "Thou wast not born for death, immortal Bird! / No hungry generations tread thee down." The pressure of negation here and the ever-shifting ambiguity of the metaphor, however, defy a singular, ameliorative, transcendent interpretation; Keats the listener cannot help but entertain contrarieties and be called back by the musical "word like a bell," back to "my sole self." Of course, we, too, are listeners or readers presented with Keats the singer, and the ambiguities of his musical metaphor resonate in our own experience as listeners and readers, enabling us to explore a conflicted fullness ourselves.

That thrilling fullness of Keats's paradoxical art is mediated always by the "self" of listener or creator. This fullness of paradox—in part his "negative capability"—is struggling always within the confines of the self, and this helps to explain the emotional tone and force of the Ode. Indeed, the Romantic use of the musical metaphor tends generally to be fixed on the tension between the outward insufficiency of the self and its inner plentitude. (The same yearning tension is, again, evident in Schubert's settings of Goethe and Muller texts.) In Keats's "Ode on a Grecian Urn," while heard melody is anxiously, even agonizingly linked to the even sweeter unheard melodies of the pure imagination, the whole metaphorical construct (and hoped-for metonymic process) remains entrapped by the dualities within the self. In this sense, too, the Romantic imagination is condemned to a sort of pained impotence, a self-consuming. Nevertheless, the musical metaphor for the Romantics, with its lease of ambiguity, its notion of a plentitude in language, of a released imagination for both creator and perceiver—all this points toward the modern and its development of the metaphor of musical dissonance.

II

The ground shared by modern and Romantic views of music is best surveyed by looking at the examples of Rousseau and Beethoven. As a precursor of the Romantic and a creator of its vision, Rousseau engages in the same consuming struggle to merge the inner and the outer. A well-noted example of how he explores the possibility for such an oceanic sense of merging is to be found in the "Fifth Promenade" of *Memoir of a Solitary Traveler*. In exile and basking on his island in Lake Geneva, he looks up to the sky and experiences the sense of harmonious oneness of self and nature apparent in other Romantic texts. Rousseau's fluid and paradoxical perception here is jointly of the disappearance of the communal self and a fullness of imaginative self. The distinctive vehicle of Rousseau's romanticism is his sharp, "enlightened" irony, an unpredictable and ambiguous play of states or selves that mixes up and ironically blends that fullness and that disappearance, images of freedom with those of imprisonment.

> If there is a state where time counts for nothing, where the present lasts forever, without marking its duration in any way, and without any trace of succession, without any other sentiment of privation, neither of enjoyment, of pleasure nor pain, of desire nor of fear, than this alone of our existence, and which this feeling alone can fill entirely: so long as this state lasts he who finds it may be called happy.[4]

Rousseau interfuses the self in nature with the self obsessed by time and society, and he ironically adjusts the focus and defines the intensity of the one image by alluding unexpectedly and continually to its negation. Rousseau here creates by negating, and that irony constitutes the essential mode of his art.

When, in his "Essay on the Origin of Language," Rousseau discusses the "language" of music, of its emotional effects freed from any connection to material experience, what emerges is an image or model of the same fertile irony. His sensitivity to negation, to the unheard melody, is the mark of his early romanticism and of his relevance to the modern. The musical process, for Rousseau, promises the perceiver not a fullness of what is but of what is not, of what is imagined. It is a type of negation, indeed of Keats's "negative capability," unashamed of self-contradiction and self-disintegration, and it is in this sense a celebration.

Music is for Rousseau a movement—like Derridian *différance*—away from stabilizing, entrapping origins toward freedom. At the core of his paradoxical conception is his notion of its play with silence, a playing that celebrates the imagination freed from bourgeois sense and presence. (These perceptions about Rousseau and music form the basis for certain extraordinary displays of deconstructive practice to be found in Jacques Derrida's *Of Grammatology* and in Paul de Man's essay of response to Derrida in *Blindness and Insight*).[5] The following is the most discursive passage of Rousseau's celebration of music's relationship to silence:

> It is one of the great advantages of the musician that he can represent things

that cannot be heard, while it is impossible to represent in painting things which cannot be seen. . . . Sleep, the calm of night, even silence enter into musical pictures.[6]

Here, in the chapter designed to correct the "false analogy between colors and sounds," between spatial and temporal form in the arts, music provides a key metaphor for Rousseau's own paradoxical "rhetorical" strategy as we saw it work in the Fifth Promenade, affirming its own revolutionary, fictive triumph over the meaningless chaos of the mechanistic moment, of the bourgeois present.

How, then, does Rousseau add to our sense of the link between the Romantic and the modern literary uses of music? To look back from the vantage of the modern at the Romantic tradition emerging from Rousseau is to be struck and disturbed by the sense of a now nearly lost imaginative spontaneity in him, the dashing and celebratory freedom of his ironies, ambiguities, negations—his performance, which is the proper and pleasurable term to describe the strategy by which his musicalized text, in Chris Norris's phrase, "survives and transcends the process of figural reduction."[7] We encountered this effect of fertility—such a performance—in the Fifth Promenade. There, his island reverie "assimilated to my fictions all the amiable objects [before me]; and finding myself brought back by degrees to myself and to what surrounded me, I could not distinguish the point of separation between fiction and reality."[8] As in the contemplation of music, the act of perception in Rousseau's work suspends all reality as potential fiction where the world of experience is not a known quantity, a mechanistic certainty, but instead a construct bound to convention and will, desire and imagination—in short, a set of fictions. It is this insight that frees for him the emotional and imaginative force of music's negative capability as well as of writing itself viewed under the aspect of music. From the vantage point of the modern period, it becomes increasingly clear that the Romantic conceptions of fiction and of music are linked: They are two names for the same process, the same striving to celebrate the freedom of individual imagination in the face of an enchaining social structure. The modern writer takes up that conception and attempts to deepen and purge it of its vestigial and mournful image of the artist's self, shackled by reality.

III

The Rousseauesque example is powerfully embodied by Beethoven, whose significance for European culture over more than a century after his death in 1827 is extraordinary, and this significance is apparent in the image of the composer and his works to be found in the writing of Proust, Mann, Forster, Huxley, Lawrence and other modern writers. Earlier, in the decades immediately after his death, it was already clear—as Leo Schrade indicates—that Beethoven's music seemed to embody for Berlioz "what Rousseau saw as music's aim: that freedom of imaginative experience particularly achieved by silence—negation."[9]

Writers from Heine on have noted the irony of fate which achieved in Beethoven's deafness a sort of freedom from the presence even of sound—the musical language's remaining tie to the world of actuality. In Heine's words, "even the invisible world of tones ceased to have any resonant reality for him."[10] Here the relationship between Romantic inwardness and outward, mundane, disillusioning reality appears even to cease to exist, or, rather, it exists only as a fiction, within the negation of silence. When, as in the Ninth Symphony, the deaf man's art seems to reclaim and affirm a colossal and contradictory fullness of human emotions, it does so ultimately and "merely" as a musical fiction, as the action of the deaf man's imagination. Mann and Proust take up this sense of Beethoven's relationship both to art and to the world of conventionalized reality, of the "human," and they locate that image of Beethoven at the focus of *Doctor Faustus* and of pages of *Remembrance of Things Past*.

Mann's novel makes Beethoven's late works a pivot for the ironic turnings of music's presence in the vision of a modern composer's and Germany's fate leading toward World War II. At one point in the novel, in the midst of the teacher Kretschmar's yearning, stuttering analysis of Beethoven's significance, the speaker is made to say that in opus 111, the last piano sonata, "the subjective and the conventional form a new relationship, conditioned by death."[11] Enclosed in "death," in the negative space of the deaf Beethoven's imagination are the great domains of both the "inner"—the subjective—and the "outer"—the conventional. Particularly the consciousness of negation—of silence and of death—in the composer's late imaginative process is crucial also to Proust. In the final volume of his novel, Proust takes up the image of the aged Rembrandt along with that of the composer of the opus 131 quartet—the late work which made Berlioz (and indeed Proust) feel "possessed by a god."[12] Proust turns the two mature artists into Schopenhauerian martyrs to the breach between art and experience, inner and outer, the subjective and the conventional. After contemplating the "terrible, grief-ravaged faces" of Rembrandt and Beethoven at the end of their lives, the narrator speculates about the connection of genius to suffering and decay:

> [L]et us submit to the disintegration of our body, since each new fragment which breaks away from it returns in a luminous and significant form to add itself to our work, to complete it at the price of sufferings . . . to make our work at least more solid as our life crumbles away beneath the corrosive action of our emotions. Ideas come to us as the successors to griefs.[13]

In the midst of Proust's obsession with the artist's mask, there are the tragic yet fertile ambiguities of his paired images—suffering and creation—which point to the decisive feature, finally the Romantic tension, in Beethoven's bearing on the modern view of music. Proust's contradictions—tensely merging and shifting between images of sorrowful experience and of fertilely constructive creativity—insist on the paradox which lies at the heart of the deaf Beethoven's example for modern literature: A purely imaginative substantiality arises amid the disintegration and disappearance of the artist's tie to the "real." Absence and death become in Beethoven's creative process inextricably joined to imaginative fullness, fertility, and freedom. The novelist's own immense work embodies this same paradoxical joining. To Theodor Adorno, Proust's art "actualizes" the promise of "hearing the unheard" and "seeing the unseen" by sensitizing us to their unattainability and absence in experience, by revealing the present impossibility of that promise: he "actualizes" this promise by "throwing it away. . . . It is the possible as promised by its impossibility. [Such] art is the promise of happiness, a promise that is constantly being broken."[14] This paradox drives to a radical conclusion the significance of the Romantic musical metaphor for modernism. How—specifically—does Beethoven's music embody this paradox?

One answer is to be found in the Hammerklavier sonata bestriding the boundary between his middle and late periods. Busoni thought it best embodied the lust of liberty—a liberated "humanity"—which

Early Romantic Ideas of Music 23

filled Beethoven "the revolutionary".[15] The Hammerklavier sonata was thought by Beethoven himself to be his greatest work for piano. This opus 106 (like opus 111 for Mann or Forster) illustrates the composer's freedom in its restructuring of sonata form and its use of "dissonance." The greatness of the sonata form itself resides partly in its unity of discipline and freedom. The discipline resides in its controlled, conventional pairing of dramatically contrasting themes and tonalities; the freedom resides in the sonata form's bold development and complications of these contrasts. When Adorno (with his influence on *Doctor Faustus*) uses the above terms, he calls attention to the "paradoxical element" implicit in the whole construct, and he emphasizes Beethoven's insistence on "the paradoxical unity" in sonata form.[16] The listener to the Hammerklavier sonata confronts such "controlled paradoxes" in each movement—in the final fugue's hammered trills and apocalyptic climaxes unifying strict counterpoint and violence, or in the exploratory freedom embodied by the fugue's introductory Largo and in the Adagio sostenuto itself, and above all in the opening Allegro's sonata exposition, in the "freed" dissonances of the development section when we hear its leaping chords modulated with a continuous abruptness—these rhythmic explosions of modulation embody simultaneously an unleashed freedom and a climax of the controlling idea of sonata development itself.[17]

The Hammerklavier sonata seems a powerfully willed acceptance of the fertility of discord and disintegration, more perhaps than it reveals what J. W. N. Sullivan hears, a tragic fury and resigned impotence.[18] Beethoven's freedom here means creating a musical text now with a consciousness of the contingency and disorder undermining its conventional language; and this freedom involves experimenting, playing with, radically developing, not despairing of or destroying that language's "constructive" forms. It is in this light of a language tested, exposed, and extended that we can best identify the searching and passionate creativity in Beethoven. Certain commentators help to clarify this vision of the composer's creativity by presenting it as an essentially Nietzschean process. There is Leo Schrade's sense in *Tragedy in the Art of Music* of Beethoven as a Prometheus, an embodiment of the tragic, Dionysian striving for "a style of art" which would project "a style of life" based in a struggling, affirmative "human ethics."[19] There is Ernst Bloch's evocation of Beethoven's defiant "passion" to transform music's language into a "dramatically form-modelling counterpoint," a passion and language that enable the listener to imagine an Antonylike self for humanity, "a truly cosmic structure so high and so deep that sun, moon, and stars could rise and set within it without colliding and there is space to encompass the whole of humanity."[20] There is Wilfrid Mellors' simpler, more tempestuous version of the "wholeness" promised and perceived in Beethoven: He becomes a sort of prophetic angel and colossus in time who is capable of returning us "to springs of unconscious life"[21] and who enables the god-playing Prospero in us to join the Caliban within, to say "this thing of darknesse I acknowledge mine." Beethoven proclaims "the identity between human and divine, between flesh and spirit."[22] Finally, Maynard Solomon offers us a careful analysis of Beethoven's power to transform the contradictions of his existence not only into reconciling beauty but into images of liberation which empower the critical freedom of his listener.[23]

These images of Beethoven, with their Nietzschean imaginings of tragic affirmation and wholeness, begin to sketch or imply an intellectual history from Beethoven to the present, a historical view based "on the assumption that music is a mirror of the intellectual life of our time" (this is Joseph Kerman's phrase in *Contemplating Music*.)[24] Kerman is characterizing particularly Leonard B. Meyer's valuable *Music, the Arts, and Ideas*, and the thesis of Meyer's study finds a sort of apotheosis in the images of Beethoven noted here.[25] Meyers proposes that meaning and value in music are especially linked to the opening up of its language to unexpected possibility, to deviation from normal order. This Beethovenian exposure and extension of musical order tests and transcends that order, and Meyer understands as well that the challenge of such music involves a form of danger, a suffering as the parameters of the listener's expectations and experience are expanded and at risk. I want now to look more closely at the paradox of conjoined possibility and danger in Beethoven's art, at the risks involved in its freedom and process: the risks of negation, of exploding or subverting the artist's language which itself exists in a state of complex tension, of balanced and barricaded paradox.

IV

How does the perceiver experience the musical tensions in Beethoven's freed variations of convention? Such tensions will illuminate the reader's encounter with modern literary texts modeled on a Beethovenian aesthetic. The music listener here engages a "full world" built (as Charles Rosen, among others, has demonstrated) from dissonances, from Beethoven's "filling out of the chromatic space."[26] Like his other variations of convention, this effort to "liberate" the tonal field involves a risk which we saw is implicit in a dissonant aesthetic and which is associated with the later New Viennese School's subversion and invalidation of art's conventional language. There is a relevant discussion of Beethoven and music in D. H. Lawrence's *Aaron's Rod* that illuminates this risk; the episode is akin to similar moments involving Philip Quarles in Huxley's *Point Counter Point* or Forster's Helen Schlegel in *Howards End* who knows "one can trust Beethoven" because he shows that the "goblins" of "panic and emptiness" coexist with his affirmations.[27] Similarly, Aaron Sisson in Lawrence's novel helps to define the risk involved in listening. Two opposed audiences for music are represented in the novel by Lady Franklin, a patroness of art, and by Aaron, the flute player and protagonist. One audience is "social" and controlled, the other individual and exploratory.

In the novel the two ways of listening, of imagining, become—after a struggle—irremediably severed one from another. For Aaron, to listen to or play Beethoven is, he says, a disturbing and "risky" experience.[28] His way of engaging music—as much as it is allowed by the leisure and liberalism of the haute bourgeoisie—is profoundly menaced, alienated, and opposed to the too-easy affirmations in Lady Franklin's way of perceiving Beethoven's music. For her, to listen to Beethoven involves the essentially social delight and solace of having her status as powerful and cultured figure affirmed, and unlike Aaron, she insulates herself against any risk, excess, or freedom beyond the bourgeois affirmation she finds of her delusion, of her brittle power.

The opposition between these two engagements of Beethoven is presupposed and shaped by the core paradox of the composer's art. As Adorno suggests, his work starting with the Eroica "explodes the schema of a complaisant adequacy of music and society."[29] Adorno describes the radical subversion here of the merely social/conventional (a subversion dear to the heart of Lawrence and central to modernism):

> If Beethoven is the musical prototype of the revolutionary bourgeoisie, he is at the same time the prototype of a music that has escaped from its social tutelage and is esthetically autonomous, a servant no longer.... That bour-

geois society is exploded by its own immanent dynamics—this is imprinted in Beethoven's music. . . . By its power, his successful work of art posits the real success of what was in reality a failure.[30]

In terms of actual bourgeois life, the Beethovenian spectacle of organic form, of living power, is a falsity. Beethoven's revolutionary freedom is a fiction that exposes the absence of human, nurturing success in the grind of the imperial machine of bourgeois power with its facade of liberal freedoms. Frederic Jameson, in his introduction to Jacques Attali's *Noise*, quotes Adorno's sentence on Beethoven as a "revolutionary Bourgeoisie . . . a servant no longer."[31] However, Jameson uncharacteristically ignores the rest, and as a result leaves out Adorno's essential critique, the key insight that Beethoven does not reconcile his listener to a totalizing order but instead "explodes" its operative myths and exposes the inadequacy of its order. Attali's deeper misunderstanding in this regard stems from the dishonoring of "risky" alienation and paradox as values in his technocratic economy of music.[32] For him, all listening is reducible to the currency of noise, and the risk of composition is engaged only when music is conceived as an obliterating of previous codes, an infinite flow of sound which is like endlessly generated capital—a fiction which charges and energizes Attali's sense of any investment or "wager," whether social or aesthetic. The mechanism is apparent here by which the "terms" and intent of critical revaluation are preempted and absorbed by the invasive, manipulative assumptions of late twentieth-century society. Attali's argument is echoed by contemporary theorists more beholden to Adorno, for example, Terry Eagleton, as well as Jameson; the approach to be found in *Noise* or, far more compellingly, in Eagleton's *The Ideology of the Aesthetic* is part of an effort generally to interrogate and discredit the tie between Romanticism and modernism.[33] Post- or "hyper-modernism"—as Adorno comments— "prefers to join forces with reified consciousness rather than stay on the side of an ideology of illusory humanness," of an alienated and dissonant consciousness.[34]

The paradoxical potency of Beethoven's own dissonant play with illusion is that his art does not merely expose but—Rousseaulike— glories in the potentiality of what Adorno calls its "esthetic untruth" of the fictive process itself.[35] The "greenest meadowlands" of exfoliating variations in opus 111 or the Ninth Symphony are cases in point—the beneficent image is Mann's homage to Adorno's father's name, woven into *Doctor Faustus* (55). The paradox in listening to such music is to experience both the celebration of a willful, powerful dynamism and the revelation of its fictionality, the sense that it is a function of a merely fictive, imaginative act. When we discover that Beethoven kept a framed motto of Isis above his desk—"I am all, what is, what was, what will be"—we face precisely that paradox which compels and disturbs.[36] D. F. Tovey illuminates that assaulting paradox when he comments on the ironic incident when Beethoven turned on the sobbing audience to his improvising and, with a mocking laugh, called them fools: "It is an outward sign of one of the highest qualities of Beethoven's spiritual grace. In a more conciliatory form it is represented by William James's profound observation that it is not good for us to be content to enjoy art passively, and that, if we cannot ourselves be artists, we must at all events not receive without giving."[37] What does Beethoven's listener give? To confront this question is to see how the process of listening is analogous to the process of reading the challenging texts of modern novelists and poets.

To listen to Beethoven, for example to the imaginative explosions of the Hammerklavier sonata, is not to receive preformed sentiments or to feel the structure of bourgeois power and perception validated. To listen is, instead, to perform a revolutionary function: to comprehend its powerful language as a creative fiction. It is to witness the fictiveness of ever-transforming structure, though structure it is nonetheless, and so to doubt fixed certainties, to engage a destabilizing, dizzying freedom of consciousness, to test and absorb and build a continual shifting and renewal of imaginative possibility. It is to be cut loose from the habitual patterns of feeling by means of our doubt and freedom and so to be drawn into the paradoxically illusory presence and process of imagining.

In an essay on Beethoven, "Musica Practica," Roland Barthes offers a related view of freedom and creativity in Beethoven and literary texts seen in the light of his music.

> The operation by which we can grasp this [feature of] Beethoven (and the category he initiates) can no longer be either performance or hearing, but reading. This means that with respect to his music one must put oneself in the position or, better, in the activity of an operator, who knows how to displace, assemble, combine, fit together; in a word . . . structure.[38]

Barthes's conception here parallels his use in *S/Z* of the terms "polyphony," "tonal instability," and the "atonality" of modern narrative[39] (Bakhtin identifies a similarly demanding "polyphony" in his analysis of Dostoyevsky's dialogic relationship to his reader). Barthes, in his essay on playing Beethoven, is indicating and indeed celebrating the imaginative process activated and liberated in the reader of the "future," as Barthes says—particularly of modern fiction. This access to freedom defines the bearing of Beethoven and of the musical metaphor itself for modern literature, and it is that liberation of creativity in the aesthetic process which is the troubled and challenging Romantic legacy for our century's practitioners of dissonance.

3
Literature and Music in the Nineteenth Century: From Schopenhauer to Wagner

I

As we trace the impact of Romanticism evolving through the rest of the nineteenth century and into the twentieth, we observe a variety of ways in which the Romantic idea of creativity and freedom in the process of listening and reading is approached. In searching for the legacy offered to the modernists by that tradition of nineteenth-century thinking, we should bear in mind Thomas Mann's comments on the connnections between philosophy and art:

> One can think in the sense of a philosopher without in the least thinking according to his sense; I mean that one can avail oneself of his thoughts—and thus can think as he would by no means have thought. Here, indeed, one thought who had read Nietzsche as well as Schopenhauer and carried the one experience over into the other, setting up the most extraordinary mixture with them. But my point is the naive misuse of a philosophy which precisely artists are "guilty" of, and which I had in mind when I said that a philosophy is often influential less through its morality or its theory of knowledge, the intellectual bloom of its vitality, than by this vitality itself, its essential and personal character—more, in short, through its passion than its wisdom.[1]

One might add that there is also the potential duplicity of philosophy, which is equally nourished by myth, that the yearning in Plato's cave to find luminous, self-sustaining, self-grounded ideas of truth amid the obscure limbo of nontruth charges the project of modern philosophy just as much as it does that tradition in modernism devoted to the symbolic image. For modern fiction writers, the duplicities are redoubled, for they practice in a musicalized form that claims to be neither overt lie nor truth, which simultaneously yearns for and questions all encompassing autonomy and truth. As Mann suggests, to examine the novelists' Schopenhauerian and Nietzschean notions of musicalized form is to be concerned less with aesthetics per se than with the "essential and personal" significance the conceptions project for these writers—and for the composers who influenced them. In this study, I trace the insights *for writers* that emerge from the nineteenth-century tradition of thought about music, which culminates in the idea of dissonance Nietzsche formulates, modern composers utilize, and modern novelists adapt in order to charge and activate their extraordinary imaginative projects.

Schopenhauer, Mallarmé, Pater in England, Wagner, and Nietzsche above all, present conceptions of music which profoundly influenced modern novelists. The impetus to use the musical metaphor stems, as we saw, from Romanticism, and it leads finally to the great musicalized structures of modern fiction, yet that development met with tortuous and revealing difficulties throughout the nineteenth century. Indeed the theorists of the period betray at times—even as they grapple toward—the notion of the perceiver's experience that Beethoven's late works assume and which finally modern fiction projects, that "sinister resonance" which "pushes" the perceiver "beyond" a conventionalized sense of actuality into the freed activity of the imagination. The legacy of nineteenth-century aesthetics for the modernists can be seen as a series of sometimes halting steps in the evolution of a challenge to the modern reader that he, in effect, become an active participant in creating the meaning of fiction.

A first such step is Schopenhauer's understanding in The *World as Will and Idea* of music's nature and value, its relationship to actual experience. Reality, in this view as in Conrad's for example, is implacably hostile to man, for it is a manifestation of the irrational Will—impossible to satisfy or comprehend and the source of the pain (and what the present century might call the absurdity) in life.[2] In his "pessimistic" and enervated recognition of the vacuum of spirit actually enclosed within the inflated structure of bourgeois power,

Schopenhauer sees the illusion of art as a sole access to a sort of wholeness and above all to resignation. The aesthetic illusion implicates—in Mann's summation—"not the head alone but the whole man, heart and sense, body and soul, and [rises] above dry reason on the one hand and idolatry of instinct on the other;" the perceiver, wracked in life by the alternative pulls of reason and instinct, is enabled by art to achieve for its space and time the will-less absence of pain.[3] Art here provides the only genuine human pleasure, for it is the only human activity not at the service of the Will's remorseless striving. Moving beyond the Romantic rhetoric of a desired merging between inwardness and the outer world, Schopenhaurer's view is yet fixed on the defeat of that desire: hence, his increased pessimism, his sense of the negativity of such artistic merging. Indeed, he defines the Romantic, oceanic possibility that the "All sings" by inverting the dichotomy of inner and outer: for him, the world itself embodies the irrational flux of feeling not as a "language" but as terrible actuality.

Music plays a crucial role in this inverting strategy for Schopenhauer (and later for the Symbolists he influenced, as A. G. Lehmann and others have demonstrated).[4] That art is seen to stand above all the others. Its pure insubstantiality is strictly contentless, freed from specific use or the "representation" of any specific phenomena, of "Ideas."[5] As a freed rendering of the flux itself of will, music offers the sole possibility of transcending the Will. A musical art becomes the crucial means for surviving the implicitly destructive disintegration in Western, bourgeois experience. That view has a significant bearing on Mann, Proust, Conrad, and other novelists; even as they move beyond its limits, their works are shaped by a similar idea of the role of art.

The example of Mann's *Buddenbrooks* clarifies both that bearing and its limits. The novel's climax presents the dying patriarch Johannes Buddenbrooks reading Schopenhauer's *The World as Will and Idea*, and places this despairing image next to that of Hanno—his son, and the last of the line in this high bourgeois family—struggling to improvise at the piano.[6] Here in the midst of a partly conventional chronicle—highly orchestrated, yet in the vein of "realism"—of a bourgeois family's decline, Mann confronts the reader with an ironic contradiction of images (this is indeed one of the recurrent, experimental formal tactics of the novel). Here it is not only that the father disapprovingly sees his son as a weak, ineffectual victim of the world of the Will, nor is it merely that the passive son's impotent music ironically reflects on the father's own impotence—his Schopenhauerian pessimism—and so, doubly seals the family's fate. The deepest contradiction of the text signals its modernity, for the reader is made to realize that the *novel's* own partly musicalized art has only a fictive fullness: it is only as art that it endures its ironic, contradictory tidings—its key leitmotifs—of utter, "actual" impotence and disintegration. The evidence of Schopenhauer's presence is everywhere here; his idea of music, his major "metaphor," defines the way in which the novel complicates and transcends its traditional role "representing" the world of merely social or moral convention and, furthermore, enables the reader imaginatively to encounter a fictive rendering of the immensely "serious," ravaging flux of generational contradiction, of "irrational" time in this bourgeois moment. However, Mann's novel—and modern fiction generally—reveals simultaneously a qualification to Schopenhauer's influence.

In the philosopher's conception, the aim of our experience as will-less perceivers of musically conceived narrative would be that we are "relieved of our suffering selves" and, so, are in resigned sympathy with the suffering of all existence. Yet the incessant irony and self-contradiction of a modern text like *Buddenbrooks* (with its mix of comedy, assured grotesqueness, and despair), or indeed *Heart of Darkness*, demand that the reader engage in a ceaseless, active process which suspends pessimistic resignation or metaphysical solace in an imaginative flux of possible interpretive responses. For the modern novel, the musical metaphor presupposes this active process of the reader's engagement. It is, finally, the passive nature of the reader's imaginative experience in Schopenhauer's conception which gives rise to a crucial ambiguity, asserted, for example, by Mann's charge that it is "life denying."[7] The ambiguous passivity—which qualifies the philosopher's influence for modernists—is clarified by a brief discussion of the context of music and literature in the period.

II

In the generation of Romantic composers after Beethoven and Schubert, there is an increasing breakdown in the unity and growth of form (though, as we saw, Beethoven's assertion of those formal qualities is ironic and confronts the listener with the recognition of how illusory and failed in bourgeois actuality is the triumphant transcendence posited by his art). The breakdown of the classical illusion of unity and growth becomes more and more overt as the nineteenth century unfolds. For Schumann—in the Davidsbündlertanze, for example, as in his essays—there is presented an aching gap, with brutal lack of transition, often only silence, between a music of easeful lyric death and the vibrant illusion of an activated will, between passages by his mythic, extroverted Florestan and those by his inward Eusebius. His music dramatizes a quasi-Schopenhauerian gulf between the passive soul and the voracious will, between the alienated, shrinking inner life enduring bourgeois society and the outer life dominated by its imperial, commodifying expansion of power. The desperation Schumann felt in the face of that gap, that silencing of the spirit, is reflected in the struggle echoed in his journalism to create a new audience of critical listeners, a "league of David" opposed to the same Philistine bourgeoisie Arnold confronted.[8]

Yet the music of Schumann and other romantics of his generation is not only a cry of protest—it is also an anatomy of the spirit. The violence and silences, the intentionally fragmented ramblings and reversals of mood contained within quasi-classical structures (sonatas, symphonies, etc.) are implicated as expressions of the problem itself: the bourgeois will's usurpation of the spirit yields a remorseful, pathos-filled yearning for a healing transcendence. Chopin's music raises similar issues, perhaps even more obviously, for the aesthetic priority of conventional harmonic order and balanced structure is even less Chopin's commitment as he alloys them with idiosyncratic folk forms, infuses them via ornament with a seductive, destabilizing chromaticism, and shapes them with a rhetoric of violence and silence, of apocalyptic gestures at moments of climax and cadence. The result is that Chopin makes more overt what Schumann struggles with: the demonic power of will to possess the spirit, to be a means of aesthetic exploration that threatens to explode aesthetic balance, to promise transcendent power as it drives the transcendent into silence. Later composers—Liszt, Berlioz, and Wagner, as we will see—drive the logic of the demonic to a radical conclusion. Their music can grip the perceiver in a strangling embrace of power and will, an aesthetic experience "of letting myself be penetrated and invaded, in a truly sensual delight resembling that of rising in the air or of revolving in the sea."[9] This apocalyptic affirmation is Baudelaire's, and the sea becomes one of his key metaphors for music's field of action.

Baudelaire's poetry is itself the scene of that partly Schopenhauerian drama. But his work also suggests ways in which music provides terms of analogy that illuminate the aims and impact on the reader of the literature he sought to create, finally a musicalized, modern literature. In "Music," for example, the speaker's spirit is shattered and flattened by the aesthetic experience of listening to music and, as the poem's original title indicates, particularly to Beethoven. Baudelaire's emphasis on the listener's experience defines part of the poet's modernity in his insistence on the ways the listener is defamiliarized by as well as a participant in the process itself of art, its reception, but also its creation. The metaphoric form itself here calls attention to the reader's participation in assembling its meaning. The image is that of a seaborne mariner (practically tied to a mast like Odysseus) encountering a storm and then still seas, and the image so dominates the poem's subject, the act of listening to music, that the subject becomes both music listener and mariner. The wavering ambiguity of this unstable image spurs the reader's work, his own creative, self-testing engagement. The poem synaesthetically encompasses these seductive, Sirenlike realms in order, finally, to celebrate and explore the inner world of image making, of emotional perception, finally a vale of soul making.

We repeatedly encounter the Sirens' song as an image for music's power—in Baudelaire, in Nietzsche, in Mallarmé, and also in Maurice Blanchot, pivotally because Blanchot's late modern conception in "The Sirens' Song" and elsewhere helps to clarify the uses of sea and music as a joint metaphorical construct, finally as a modernist aesthetic. In discussing the archetypal encounter of Ulysses and the Sirens, Blanchot shows how the Sirens' call obscurely permeates Ulysses's sense of ordered, ordinary reality, the Sirens' song arising imperfectly into hearing, a lure of musicality, a wavering nothingness, a hypnotic fiction.[10] "Through their imperfect song . . . they lured the navigator towards the space where singing really begins."[11] The sea itself is the scene of the lure and birthing of such imaginary song, for its endless water reinforces the hearer's sense of the features of the fictive music: how it connects one to the billowing potentiality for the imaginary, to a continuous flow of wonder and transcendence, but also to the terror and endless flux and wandering uncertainty of navigating the processes of the imaginary. The inevitable incompleteness of perception in the face of the sea's endlessness leads us back to Blanchot's emphasis on the imperfection of all heard melody. What I have called dissonance is, in Blanchot's terms, this imperfection of song, the inbuilt silence in the song-text of modernity. This dissonant awareness leads to the practice of narrative as the key modernist genre. "When writing becomes acceptance of endlessness," Blanchot suggests in "The Essential Solitude,"[12] "the writer who bears the burden of its specificity relinquishes the right to say 'I.'" For example, "Kafka discovered literature when he was able to replace 'I' by 'he,'" to replace the authorial *I*'s lyric certainties with the narrative *he*'s endless fictive possibilities. And here the reader joins the writer in experiencing the lure and dizziness, the power and terror, of the musically conceived text.

Baudelaire's own beautiful and disintegrating lyrics are the scene of such vertiginous attraction, of the Sirens' song. To return to his self-reflexive "Music," the listener/reader's working through that lure and dizziness is profoundly self-searching, bringing the lyric I to the point of exhaustion, so that for Baudelaire the first person itself begins the metamorphosis that Blanchot describes. In the poem's climax, the I becomes the subject of self-disintegration, indeed subject to the self-indictment of his own reflexive mirroring of modernity's malaise: "Level calms come silvering sea and air, / A glass for my despair."[13] A soul-flattening silence of spirit—ennui—is the assaulting message of the spirit in bourgeois life, as another poem, "To the Reader," equally suggests: "How well you know this fastidious monster, reader, / —Hypocrite reader, you!—my double! my brother!"[14]

The same assault in the work of Baudelaire's key contemporary, Flaubert, is informed by a paradoxical sense like Blanchot's of the endless possible gradations here of irony and sympathy in third person narrative, as well as by an understanding like Baudelaire's of the musical analogy for literature generally and its alluring and subversive effect on the reader. The most assaulting experiment in *Madame Bovary* is the country fair scene, and musical terms are often used to describe it. In a letter to Louise Colet, Flaubert himself speaks of "the effects like those of a symphony" he sought for the competing, orchestrated voices of the scene,[15] and criticism has since found there a counterpoint of voices. To the extent that these voices clash and destabilize the reading process, there is a dissonant counterpoint to be heard—as when the cliché-mired Rudolf courts the "romantically" hungry Emma, while the similarly cliché-stiffened official shouts his awards:

> "First prize for general farming!" announced the president.
> "—Just now, for example, when I went to your home...."
> "To Mr. Bizet of Quincampoix."
> "—Did I know I would accompany you?"
> "Seventy francs!"
> "—A hundred times I tried to leave; yet I followed you and stayed...."
> "For manures!"
> "—As I would stay tonight, tomorrow, all other days, all my life!"[16]

In such a narrative structure, the key effect is that of ironic assault which achieves the dissonance, the "sinister resonance" Conrad describes. The entwined parody of voices confronts the reader with the task of critically assessing and enduring the failure to create even the echo of meaningful expression through the scene's bourgeois gestures of sentiment and community, and Flaubert's dissonant text confronts us with our own complicity—caught between irony and sympathy—as we witness how "the human tongue is like a cracked cauldron on which we beat out tunes to set a bear dancing when we would make the stars weep with our melodies."[17]

In the music of the mid-nineteenth century, as well, we find the same extremity of assaulting irony and yearning. Certain scores reveal the "demonic" energy latent in the interstices of bourgeois life; their essential musical gestures reflect the inflation of power shaping mid-century culture as it falsifies and destroys any meaning beyond the realm of power and commodity. With Berlioz and Liszt, the bourgeois listener is often confronted with that demonic, abusively parodying energy that simultaneously projects and ironizes the cheap audacity and vacancies of the inner life in that culture. In Liszt's "Mephisto Waltz," for example, the self-implicating anxiety (and even revulsion) of the listener is a response to an instability in the work; the distinction is blurred in it between an exaggerated, vulgar projection of power and sentiment and an ironic exposure of their emptiness. The audience is arrested on the border between acquiescence and censure—ultimately self-censure. The crisis for art after about 1850 is in part precisely this crisis for the audience, unable to create meaning beyond such gestures. This fracturing of the "creative spirit" reflects the experience, of course, of the composer as well—here Liszt, who played the Hammerklavier sonata and the Hungarian Rhapsodies on the same program. The self-destructive frenzy and brittleness of mid-century music is the immediate result of that crisis in meaning and form which does not then cease for Western art. By the 1870s, two approaches to the crisis in both music and literature had emerged (a third, modern resolution had yet fully to emerge, the development beyond Flaubert of an encompassing fiction infused with world-testing irony). One approach then was the Lisztian (and later we will see, the Wagnerian) confrontation of the audience with its own demonic seduction, reduced to both bourgeois violence to the spirit, and a mythic banality. The other approach we turn to now is the flight from banality toward the symbol, into a pure musicality, the way of Axel and Mallarmé and—in music—Debussy.

III

The aesthetic developed by Mallarmé, the central poet and theoretician of symbolism, is shaped by the Schopenhaurian assumptions and their limitations. In his essay "Music and Literature" and elsewhere, Mallarmé lays the groundwork for a formalist belief that poetry ought to achieve music's self-sustaining transcendence of modern reality. Poetry should imitate music's "playful," suggestive, and—in terms of content—infinitely ambiguous evocation of feeling's form.[18] This article of Symbolist faith suggests both the power and the limits of the aesthetic, particularly in its influence on Joyce and Proust. The power of the conception is partly to heighten a sense of the potency in the musical metaphor for literature. Beyond the Romantic yearning for a harmonious merging of inner and outer worlds, Mallarmé's musicalized art becomes the encompassing language not merely for humanist desire or its inversion in irony and banal parody.

The musical transformation of poetry above all yields, for Mallarmé, a language initiating the reader into a vast symbolic continuum, imagining the flux of pure ambiguity, the obscure and irrational: "A throw of the dice] will never annul chance." In the fully, self-consciously musicalized "A Throw of the Dice," we return to the Sirens' world; here the navigator—reader/listener/creator—floats in suspension amid waves of poetry, indeed floats amid the singing, contrapuntal, clashing and insubstantial waverings of sound and type, floats free in the midst of the shipwreck of being, free of all destiny in being.[19] Musicalized form is now cut loose from "reality" which is seen as a ravaged cliché, a moribund fiction. "Music again and always" reads Verlaine's "Ars Poetica."[20] And from this font of the symbol flows Mallarmé's infinitely allusive string quartet or symphony in words. "All the rest is literature." And arising from the same aesthetic synthesis of the musical and the verbal is Dujardin's symbolist novel, prefiguring Joyce's early work. His internal monologue aims to achieve music's "simultaneity, its development in time."[21] Dujardin, as a symbolist novelist, thought of his musical fiction as a quasi-religious elevation of inner time, and this conception partly prefigures Proust's vision of the moments of spiritual time which enliven and redeem the chaotic, mechanized, habitual flux of "real" experience.

Yet, to mention Proust in connection with the Symbolists is to remind us of the limited ability of their aesthetic to account for the radical masterpieces of modern fiction. When a Mallarméan music aspires to a sensuous and ambiguous "evocation, allusion, and suggestion," the result can be the artifice of blockage and enervation produced by fin de siècle literature. Where the modern novel seeks to confront the reader with a fictive plundering of experience, a world-rivaling fiction, in contrast the purely symbolist art withdraws from such an encompassing imaginative engagement of the disintegrating bourgeois world and uses musicalized art not as an instrument in the service of that fictive plundering and creation, but rather as a means to "dream," infused with Mallarmé's hope in "Music and Literature" that "the mind may seek its own native land again" and poetry be "received" into the realm of music.[22] For the Symbolist, the reader's role is to explore that dreamlike inner region which Mallarmé would see discovered in "the reader's imagination" itself. What results is the contemplation of "lyric forms of pure musicality"—the self-sufficient expressivity of an inner state. Mallarmé here seeks, as Jean-Pol Madou suggests, a mythic kingdom of nonbeing,[23] yet this Symbolist search is simultaneously a withdrawal from the dynamic and profound engagement of the reader yielded by *À la recherche du temps perdu* or *Ulysses*. Françoise Meltzer comments on the poet's use of the image of Salome are apposite to his musicalized text; Mallarmé's subversion of the dance as a metaphor for writing questions all that presumes to be automatic and conventional and referential in writing's manipulation of illusion: "If Mallarmé succeeds in deautomatizing writing, it is by admitting that there is no dance, and no woman dancing."[24] Rendered in dissonant forms which question their own vital and alienated illusion, colossal images of men and women yet dance through Proust's and Joyce's musicalized texts.

The strengths and weaknesses I have been examining in the Symbolist aesthetic can be located as well in the contemporaneous work of Walter Pater. His ideas—together with Arthur Symons's influential expression both of them and of the Symbolists'—form a crucial part of the cultural milieu within and against which novelists in English—Joyce, Lawrence, Woolf, Forster, and Conrad among them—defined their art. In Pater's classic description of music's value in *The Renaissance*, he presents the formal, symbolist ideal of music's pure expressivity:

> It is the art of music which most completely realizes the artistic ideal of the perfect identification of matter and form. In its consummate moments, the end is not distinct from the means, the form from the matter, the subject from the expression.[25]

Conrad and Joyce move beyond the limits of this conception, yet their views of music, and the later novelist's youthful celebration of the rhythm phrase as the perfect mode of literary expression, echo Pater's statement and his style of polished abstraction, repetition, and passive-voiced ambiguity.

Pater's style—its obscure, incantatory yearning for a vaguely expressed alternative to demeaned, prosaic reality—renders perfectly the ambiguity of his meaning. What is Pater's central ambiguity, the source of both his power and his limitations? His idea of music as a model for art's "consummate moments" obscures the distinction between the aesthetic form and the "aesthetic life." The living subject and the formal expression are identical, Pater implies, and indeed should equally "burn with a hard, gemlike flame."[26] The "Conclusion" to *The Renaissance*, which most fully develops this ambiguity, seems at times to mistake surface for depth, the presence of sensation for the process of the imagination. Yet it is partly as a result of this characteristic obscuring of realms that Pater's best work achieves an "appreciation" particularly of the human costs exacted by that partly Romantic pursuit of the imagination. His classic passage on "La Giaconda" (a self-conscious piece of prose music, indeed, which Yeats chose for the opening of his edition of the *Oxford Book of Modern*

Poetry) disturbingly projects the imaginative process through which Mona Lisa's body and smile simultaneously become and consume all history and humanity, at once sacred and profane: "As Leda, [she] was the mother of Helen of Troy, and, as Saint Anne, the mother of Mary; and all this has been to her but as the sound of lyres and flutes."[27] The entire passage illustrates his understanding of the self-consuming evanescence and contradiction implicit in the aesthetic process he admires, and he turns his idiosyncratic yet penetrating insight into a celebration of the defiantly inexhaustible playfulness of the greatest art.

Pater's sense of the ambiguous process by which life and art may be musically conjoined is taken up and transformed by Conrad and Joyce. Their situation is suggested by Yeats's remark that the Paterian aesthetic taught his generation to "walk upon a rope, tightly stretched through serene air, and we were left to keep our feet upon a swaying rope in a storm."[28] The most ambitious modern novelists in English—like Yeats himself, but in narrative rather than elegy or love lyric—transformed their subsequent fall to earth, into the matter of fiction. They transform Pater's aesthetic into a strategy (freed of obsession with—though aware of—its costliness) by which the novel challenges the reader to explore its fictive absorption of the modern world. That strategy—of dissonance—takes up the ambiguities of the Paterian musical metaphor as a means to achieve a full and open-ended fictive encounter with imaginative experience, an encounter which—in Pater's later view—is the aim of great art. However, in the period of late nineteenth-century aestheticism, Pater's ambitious yet disguised conception became a rationale for a style of overwrought, gemlike effects, as well as for a Wildean self-fabrication—a consuming, enraged dream of the self. Joyce and Conrad view with transfiguring irony—and certainly at times self-irony—that paradoxical legacy of symbolism which Pater independently brought to English literature.

IV

The composer who is a central part of that complex legacy is Wagner, and his thought and art can help us more precisely define the ambiguous value to modern novelists of the late nineteenth-century idealization of music. Wagner was—in Mann's words—"the most glorious brother and comrade of all the sufferers from life, given to pity, seeking for transport, these art-mingling symbolists, worshippers of l'art suggestif"—above all, of music.[29] Within this symbolist, Wagnerian brotherhood, we again find Dujardin. The novelist, who edited the *Revue Wagnerienne,* was additionally attracted to Wagnerian opera because its extended forms spoke, in part like the genre of fiction itself, to and of a culture and a people. For Dujardin, Wagner's use of the leitmotif was an exemplary disintegration and restructuring of traditional form, and it—with the "endless melody" of Wagner's chromaticism—provided the self-conscious model for his experimental *monologue intérieur.*[30] Wagner's influence on later novelists stirred in them a qualified yet strategic admiration (his influence has been well chronicled, for instance by S. P. Sher's survey and by John Louis DiGaetani's book-length study).[31] With rich ambiguity Proust weaves *Tristan* and *Parsifal* into the great tapestry of his novel. Joyce's youthful and earnest Ibsen essay exemplifies the ambiguity of the influence; it appropriates Wagner as an exponent of the dramatic form which then the mature novelist, of course, turns to unexpectedly ironic and liberated use.[32] There is also Mann's signal celebration of the significance and spectacle in Wagner's "suffering and greatness," as well as the German novelist's early regard, yet finally also his later irony for the use of leitmotif and his varied judgment of Wagner's innovative approach to dissonance.[33]

Given the notion of music's significance for modern fiction which I am exploring, a central basis of qualification to Wagner's influence concerns the question of the perceiver's experience of his opera. Baudelaire's account (which I earlier excerpted) of hearing one of the first performances of *Tristan und Isolde* establishes key features of the listener's reception of Wagner:

> I felt myself freed from the bonds of gravity.... Then I realized to the full the idea of a soul moving in a luminous environment, of an ecstasy consisting of delight and knowledge.... I experienced the pride and climactic joy of understanding, of letting myself be penetrated and invaded, in a truly sensual delight resembling that of rising in the air or of revolving in the sea.[34]

This early and brilliant listener draws primarily on the sensuous imagery of passion—its seductions, its confusion of self with object, its pervasive sexualizing of the "environment." That imagery celebrates his imaginative release into a world of irrational will, as if the listener, too, imbibes the love potion of the opera. The chromatic dissonance of Isolde's primary leitmotif, which dominates the opera from its opening chords, is the emblem of potion and passion, embodying and enacting their significance, their breaking of the bonds of tonal and social convention. The resulting access to passion is simultaneously a strangling excess. What the listener experiences is ambiguously both a beautiful, "freed" activation of feeling and its "drowning" and invasive compulsion, at one and the same time a joyous release and a sort of Schopenhauerian passivity before the spectacular and ravaging equation of passion with death. It is the reader's passivity as the instrument of such an equation that first Mallarmé, and then the modernists who follow him, repudiate in favor of a "musicality" which frees as it engages "the imagination of the reader."[35]

Wagner's own conception of the listener's role seems, at least on the surface, to involve no such passivity of the individual perceiver in the grip of the will. Instead, he saw in the *Ring* "an appeal to the feelings of the people," as he wrote in "The Art Work of the Future."[36] Through opera, Wagner would mythologize the emotions felt by the national mass of Germans. Wagner asserts here that his art would be "religion brought to life," transforming the emotional life of "humanity" into a "mythic cry." He wanted, in other words, to give voice and religious, mythic sanction to what Schopenhauer posited art renders and transcends, the instinctual will of a race. Yet, more deeply, the life and death of that will finally becomes a presence—the Wagnerian myth—which would put an end to the perceiver's activity of individually testing his perceptions, to the play of ambiguity, to the fictive, dissonant process which we have seen has otherwise marked the promise and significance of the musical metaphor. Nietzsche writes in *The Case of Wagner* that the listeners of nineteenth-century Europe, "in Paris . . . in St. Petersburg," are swept up by the mania for Wagner, by a music which in part betrays their capacity for critical growth; this phenomenon—in which he himself participated—indicates "how closely related Wagner must be to the whole of European decadence to avoid being experienced by them as a decadent. . . . One honors oneself when raising him to the clouds!"[37] The underlying point here is that Wagner wants his music—not only as performed in Bayreuth—to hold the perceiver in its embrace. This is the case when he absorbs symphonic strategies into his dramatic manipulations (a brilliant melding of theater, myth, and music which Kerman's *Opera as Drama* discusses),[38] and also when he glorifies the inner world of suffering and transport, or when he transforms "the people's" feelings into a fateful, essentially bourgeois myth of power and community. Wagner's listener is the "fulfilled" yet fundamentally still passive recipient of the music's embrace, the grasp of a solacing, fabricated myth as a newly created "reality."

In the midst of the investment of feeling, comprehension, and time which Wagner's works require, that essential and peculiar passivity of his listener forms a contrast to the freed, exploratory listening activity which Beethoven's art assumes and requires, as Bloch, Barthes, and others confirm. Wagner's music does not activate the critical independence on which that liberating process of "ontological music" depends, as Bloch suggests; it was Beethoven who "pursued this latter course, with virile, courageous, morally objective energy."[39] The peculiar passivity of Wagner's absorbed listener is finally the emanation rather than confrontation of an ultimately imperial bourgeois "ideology." Of this musical strategy involved not only in Wagner, Adorno's more general observation (which I noted in chapter 1) is that such passivity of reception takes root within "the deceptive moment" in which the "self-limited" listener seems "in accord with all, accepted by and reconciled by all"; in this way, it "fulfills men in themselves, to train them for consent."[40] And finally such music sanctions "an irrationality" which seems to have "no consequences for the demands of civilization"—except that it invests a people's cultural myth (its totalized, potentially totalitarian mass) with a felt, complaisant legitimacy. Adorno's critique of the modern, passive audience (created first and foremost perhaps by Wagner) takes up Freudian, Marxist, and Nietzschean elements, and it is of course Nietzsche who, toward the end of the nineteenth century, self-consciously and radically formulated the crucial critique of Wagner, and of music generally, which most influenced modern novelists.

4
Music and the Modern Imagination: Nietzsche and Schoenberg

I

Nietzsche is the conclusive nineteenth-century figure for the study of music's tie to modernism, and in this regard he is, next to Beethoven, the most significant, not only for his influence on individual novelists like Proust, Lawrence, and Mann, but for his seminal ideas about dissonance and its tie to listening and reading, and to modern existence itself.

One key to Nietzsche's ideas about music is suggested by his late reflections "contra Wagner," his postulating there that his own writings rather than Wagner's operas were the true focus of his early conceptions of music in *The Birth of Tragedy*.[1] Here, as well as in his 1886 preface to his early work, and in *The Wagner Case*, Nietzsche's late comments abrasively confront and—in their athletic vigor—triumph over what he saw as the decadence of Wagner's operas, the music's "surrender" to passive "impotence" and "hatred against life."[2] Wagner's listener becomes a central target of this critique: His listener is numbed to independent perception, to the needed, tragic and playful questioning. The operas achieve "effects . . . in the service, the slavery, of poses" in order "to give the people satisfaction," to "impress" them, so that ultimately the listener is "comforted metaphysically."[3] The effect, then, of Wagner's art is one of "surrender," of "floating," of "hebetation" on the passive "mass, on the immature, on the blasé, on the sick, on the idiots, on Wagnerians."[4]

The rhetorical thrust of Nietzsche's critique of the listener's "surrender" in Wagner is to call for an alternative way of engaging aesthetic experience based on radical doubt about ordinary habits of perceiving works of art. Theodor Adorno helps us to describe that doubt. A consenting passivity in the music listener, he writes, "serves the status quo, which could be changed only by people who, instead of confirming themselves and the world, would reflect critically on the world and on themselves."[5] In Nietzsche's work, music—revalued as a metaphor—can become an instrument to identify and stimulate that active, critically reflective doubt.

Before we examine the conception of music to be found in *The Birth of Tragedy* and elsewhere, let me describe generally the nature of Nietzschean doubt in music. Rather than a Wagnerian, manipulative cynicism that, to Nietzsche, seems to secure and reinforce a passivity in the "spectator," Nietzsche desires a "pessimism of strength," which can arise from the musical experience and which comprehends as well as confirms "the fullness of existence."[6] Both in aesthetic experience and in "life," consciousness and language—through which it knows itself—are redefined as activities filled with imaginative potentiality, a play of possibilities continually on the verge of coming into being. Arising from this redefinition of consciousness are critical recognitions both of the disfiguring and imprisoning hold which cliché can have over perception and of the relative "fictiveness" of "truth." Yet Nietzsche's radical and affirming pessimism emerges from, and itself yields, a sense of the overabundance and vitality of consciousness.

As we read Nietzsche's own texts, we confront a rhetoric—or really a process—which has an impact not unlike that detected by listeners as diverse as Tovey, Mann, Bloch, and Barthes in Beethoven's late works: We experience a disruption of complaisant "certainties" which is not cynical but rather looses in us a creative process and potentiality. The radical doubt with which Nietzsche assaults the reader compels in him a sense of the open-ended abundance of fiction, so that the text becomes, finally, the scene of intense activity in the reader. What such a text requires is embodied and defined by an important entry (no.310) on the wave and "we who will" from *The Gay Science*. This passage takes up a key image of sea and swimmer/navigator which has recurred in the texts on music I have examined, and it is akin also to another passage in Nietzsche's work—on the image of woman stirring the menaced recognition of life as a fiction, amid "the flaming surf"—which Derrida takes up in *Spurs* as part of his critical performance on Nietzsche.[7]

> How greedily this wave approaches, as if there were some objective to be reached! How with awe-inspiring haste it crawls into the inmost nooks of the rocky cliff! It seems that it wants to anticipate somebody; it seems that something is hidden there, something of value, high value.
>
> And now it comes back, a little more slowly, still quite white with excitement—is it disappointed? But already another wave is approaching, still greedier and wilder than the first, and its soul too seems to be full of secrets and the lust to dig up treasures. Thus live the waves—thus we who will.[8]

This destabilizing metaphorical leap from the waves to the way we live evokes how the shore of our consciousness is confronted by an overfull, vertiginous choice of imaginative possibility; the leaping vigor of Nietzsche's own text aims to provoke "us," his readers, with a wrenched and greedy liberation from habitual thinking, with "waves" of self-questioning and freedom. "The danger for the reader," David Allison suggests, "ultimately lies in the dispossession of his own identity and the loss of his conventional world."[9] Nietzsche's texts confront the bourgeois "self" in the reader with its tendency to identify with the power of the will, and they stir a transformation of that tendency by means of their critical and satiric instability. To engage the aphoristic attack particularly of his late style, its hyperbole, parody, and oxymoronic ambiguity—in short, to read Nietzsche—is, finally, to engage an intimate assault on and opening up of consciousness.

The distinction between the perceiving consciousness—with its manifestation in "style"—and the perceived "world" is erased for Nietzsche; both present themselves as a "play of appearances," an interactive abundance of fictions, finally as "waves" of language. They emerge so partly because the habitual fictions or codes—which form how and what we know—are subject to the workings of desire, to our creative will (as Gilles Deleuze argues in his discussion of Nietzsche's politics of desire).[10] What results is a suspension of consciousness and the world *as fictions*, as "texts." Nietzsche's notion of self-overcoming mirrors this conception of consciousness, for it celebrates a process of the provisional, committed creation and testing of versions of selves.[11] The idea of how "overcoming" operates illuminates the workings of Nietzsche's own text—and of modern narrative, I would add—on and for the reader. The process of testing and creating selves is the process into which the modern novel initiates the reader; such fiction self-consciously promises and welcomes the playful vitality of the process as it affirms its tragic endlessness and uncertainty. To read such a text is to navigate the disaster of modernity, to preserve access to creative freedom, and to resist the totalizing structures—or horizon—of assurance; "reading," Derrida suggests about this Nietzschean strategy, "is to perforate such an horizon or the hermeneutic sail."[12] Nietzsche's text powerfully invites this critical engagement as it eludes definitive interpretation.

Nietzsche's link to the assumptions underlying Deconstruction is worth examining here and can help us to understand some of the implications of Nietzsche's thought for dissonant narrative and for modernism itself. The work of Paul de Man, for example, offers a sometimes discomfiting appropriation of Nietzsche along with, indeed, a panoply of pre-, proto-, and postmodernisms. The dense, obscure abstraction of de Man's discourse, even the brief early invocations of racist elitism, and then the later risk of solipsism in his interpretations—all bespeak the tense importation into his work of certain, at times deformed, practices of modernism. The tortuous abstraction in de Man's presentation of these various strands of thought enacts the dilemma of a critical practice on the edge of nihilism; the agony of its circuitous refusal to affirm anything beyond its own practice in language mirrors the agony of a disappearing humanism in the aftermath of modernity.

Several essays of de Man take up Nietzsche's thought, most notably in *Allegories of Reading*, in which the emphasis is on exposing the disordered freedom of consciousness at work particularly in the most prescriptive Nietzschean rhetoric and texts.[13] This approach to Nietzsche grows from de Man's allegiance to two contradictory strains in modernist thinking: One is concerned with the agonized risk and fertility of a freed, open-ended consciousness, and the other is concerned with the purely linguistic autonomy of modernist form.

About the first, more clearly Nietzschean conception, de Man develops an idea of reading—and interpretation—as an opportunity to circumvent the "self" and the "self"-deception or "blindness" assumed by the reader's "knowledge" and values, his epistemological and methodological perspective. In this way, de Man argues for literature's power to enact and achieve the Nietzschean insight in *Ecce Homo* that "to become what one is, one must not have the faintest notion what one is."[14] "The text," de Man writes in *Blindness and Insight*, "brings the reader back to what he might have been before he shaped himself into a particular self."[15] In this derivative conception, the reader experiences a version of Binneswanger's "fall upwards," an always incomplete and unstable process, a movement out of the structured representations of empirical or metaphysical "reality" onto the plain of freed, imaginative consciousness.[16] Particularly modern literature offers the moments of "unbearable" pressure in this way to renew alternative selves, to activate the imagination.[17]

Simultaneously at work, however, in de Man's conception is a contradictory assumption that abjures all ethical resonance in literature. De Man emphasizes that literary language does not "represent" reality or any access to "meaning," but is rather a projection of purely fictive possibility, empirical only in rejecting the claims of "presence" and certainty as meaningless. In various essays, de Man adapts and indeed reduces ideas of music developed by Rousseau or Rilke or Nietzsche to a demonstration that literature—specifically a musicalized literature—demystifies and negates all "truth" claims in a process of continual, fictive construction and deconstruction. Human reality, whether critical, creative, or empirical, becomes in de Man's hands, a shallow, debased version of the scene and drama Nietzsche brilliantly describes, as follows: "Truth" is

> a mobile army of metaphors, metonyms, and anthropomorphisms—in short, a sum of human relations, which have been enhanced, transposed, and embellished poetically and rhetorically and which after long use seem firm, cannonical, and obligatory to a people: truths are illusions about which one has forgotten that this is what they are.[18]

De Man, however, in emphasizing a quasi-tragic reduction of literature into pure figuration, solely into the language of tropes, "isolates too purifyingly" (as Harold Bloom suggests) "the trope from the topos or commonplace that generates it."[19] De Man's tendency is to withdraw from the Nietzschean insistence on truth as a struggling "sum of human relations," of "people," yet "these are," as Jonathan Arac writes, exactly "the elements, less than the figures, from which to construct a history of the contingencies that have put us in the odd place that we are."[20]

It is in a struggle to understand "the odd place that we are" that Nietzsche himself creates a rhetoric to explore the sense of the endless multiplicity, contradiction, and nontruth of "truth." In this way, he offers us a prototype for modern narrative texts. Given the skepticism and freedom at work in such texts, the critical Nietzschean aim becomes to envision—as Erich Heller writes, echoing Zarathustra— what it is like to perceive and live without belief in truth, again not cynically, but with the awareness that "truth" is a function of will, judgment, self-critical sublimation, and choice.[21]

II

We can now return to the issue of the activity—as opposed to the passivity—of the aesthetic consciousness and to Nietzsche's use of the dissonant metaphor to characterize that activity. It is Nietzsche's development of that analogy which explains and prefigures the musicality—the dissonance—of the modern novel.

Nietzsche takes up the matter of music in *The Birth of Tragedy from the Spirit of Music* and then implicitly in *Thus Spoke Zarathustra*. The latter work unfolds on many levels under the aegis of the musical metaphor: "Perhaps the whole of Zarathustra may be reckoned as music," Nietzsche writes in *Ecce Homo*, and he adds a salient point about the Dionysian listener/reader: "Certainly a rebirth of the art of *hearing* was among its preconditions."[22] Nietzsche's 1886 introduction to *The Birth of Tragedy* also reminds us of Zarathustra's tie to the work of 1872.

In this early major text, he presents the fundamental idea that Greek tragedy emerged from the tension between the Apollonian and the Dionysian: the former manifests itself as the perfected, dreamlike heroic forms of tragedy, which imagine the desired ideals in "existence," and the latter is the Dionysian, "choric" response embodying the audience's emotional reaction to tragedy, the force of their awed, enraged, and immense desire for the perfected Apollonian forms.[23] To maintain the balance between Apollo and Dionysus, is the process—and finally the ascetic ideal of "overcoming"—at the core of Nietzsche's vision generally, as Arthur Danto argues.[24] Here, in Greek tragedy, the disillusioning, anarchic, "tragic insight" of the musical, Dionysian imagination—with its capacious desire for and summoning up of Apollonian forms—is the choric audience's recognition that beautiful Apollo is but a fiction yet, as such, a crucial source of the "multifarious diversity" seen as fictions, as metaphors.[25] Here the perceiver's recognition (like the creator's) denies all certainty of self, of subject, and of audience itself, in other words, moves away from the lyric ideal toward the model of dissonance. Nietzsche's conception of dissonance provides a key analysis of this Dionysian response of the perceiver in tragic art. The passage on dissonance occurs at the end of *The Birth of Tragedy,* after his celebration of the Dionysian vision he has already located in Wagner; it is one of the moments in the text when, in retrospect, we see Nietzsche wrest himself free of his anxious projection of a Nietzschean image onto Wagner's operas. Now he links musical dissonance to the phenomenon in Greek tragedy of facing the terrible, out of an overfullness of life, and of having the capacity to render and to affirm it as part of the abundance of life.

Here, the Dionysian is not seen as rooted in a Schopenhauerian "metaphysical solace" which substitutes the presence and witness of irrational "truth" for a Socratic "rationalization" of the "truth." Rather, Nietzsche's redefinition now insists that the Dionysian is an aesthetic activity, above all a process involving the listener/reader in a journey of engagement, the destination of which is unknown:

> Existence and the world seem justified only as an aesthetic phenomenon. In this sense, it is precisely the tragic myth that has to convince us that even the ugly and disharmonic are part of an artistic game that will in the eternal amplitude of its pleasure plays with itself. But this primordial phenomenon of Dionysian art is difficult to grasp, and there is only one direct way to make it intelligible and grasp it immediately: through the wonderful significance of *musical dissonance.* . . . The joy aroused by the tragic myth has the same origin as the joyous sensation of dissonance in music. The Dionysian, with its primordial joy experienced even in pain, is the common source of music and tragic myth.[26]

Musical dissonance becomes here a metaphor for the creative process activated within the freed consciousness (a "singing Socrates" indeed). Dissonance—the ambiguous movement away from and between tonal "certainties"—exists in a state of suspension, of striving beyond "heard harmony" toward its negation, the powerful, unheard creative silence which each of the writers studied here finds and celebrates in Beethoven. Dissonance—which longs "to get beyond all hearing"—"reveals to us the playful construction and destruction of the individual world as the overflow of a primordial delight."[27]

Nietzsche here moves beyond affirming the solemn myth in Wagner which holds the listener in the grasp of "metaphysical solace" and "surrender." To see this feature of the text most clearly, Walter Kaufmann shows, *The Birth of Tragedy* should be read in conjunction with excised portions and notes and particularly with the contemporaneous fragment "On Music and Words" (appended to Carl Dahlhaus's *Between Romanticisim and Modernism*),[28] a fragment which, as Dahlhaus indicates, "contains the outlines of Nietzsche's later critique of Wagner."[29] Read in this way, *The Birth of Tragedy* "explodes" the limitations of its sporadic, lyrical, "Wagnerian" affirmations, of the text's "authority," so that the Dionysian *process* at work here is shown to concern not a mythic presence but the disordered freedom of consciousness. This movement redefining the Dionysian not as solemn, irrational "truth" but as a process, finally, of liberation, is carried further in the 1886 preface criticizing the turgid lack of musicality in *The Birth of Tragedy* (which was, after all, his Ph.D. thesis). The Preface avows the need to "dance," to "learn to laugh" as essential to the nature of music, to Dionysian "play."[30] The rhetoric of modern narrative is forecast by this rhetoric of the 1886 preface, with its own experimental "dance" intermingling "critical irony and tragic gaiety, earned by that irony," very much like the autobiographical, literary strategy of *Ecce Homo* as Altieri describes it (such an aesthetic strategy pervades Nietzsche, as Alexander Nehamas shows).[31]

Modern consciousness and narrative, and finally history itself (as Foucault suggests about Nietzsche)[32] can all be understood as emanations of such dissonance. The link for Nietzsche between a dissonant aesthetic and ethic becomes evident here, and we can now also begin to see the connection between Dionysian dissonance and other keys to Nietzsche's thought—the idea of self-overcoming, as I noted earlier, and that of the eternal return. These Nietzschean ideas link together, as Kathleen Higgins has argued, to convey a "simultaneous awareness of past and present [finally projecting] a sense of the whole in which the present moment is the immediately experienced part."³³ She explains, using and then moving beyond a Zuckerkandlian perspective, that Nietzsche reveals how "we enjoy the fullness of the present musical moment, even if it is dissonant, not for its efficiency in moving towards the evident musical goal, but for its own surprising presence."³⁴ Pierre Klossowski similarly and even more insistently shows that this network of linkages (eternal return, self-overcoming, and, I would add, musical dissonance) shares an ethic and aesthetic which, above all, posit the flux of *multiplicity* in selves and events.³⁵ Nietzsche's tragic affirmation of that multiplicity is nowhere more evident than in his embrace of *amor fati*, of the eternally recurrent process by which the encompassing flux of image and experience is tested and affirmed, now, as it were, intrinsically worthy of fated reperformance. This notion of the embrace of multiplicity and "reperformance" points again to the connection I am exploring between Dionysian dissonance and the modern novel; for, in this regard, the eternal return and dissonance provide a model for reading itself. The engagement, testing, and affirmation of the ever-changing, clashing, and unfolding waves of multiplicity define that opportunity and operation of reading modern narrative. (Claude Lévesque speaks in similar terms of the tie, in the century since Nietzsche, between dissonance and aesthetic language generally.³⁶)

III

The connection between Dionysian dissonance and the modern novel can be illustrated in D. H. Lawrence's vision, in *Aaron's Rod*, which we saw presents an image of Beethoven as well, or later in *Apocalypse*, which is in part a lapsed, English "nonconformist's" variation on themes from Nietzsche's *Genealogy of Morals*.³⁷ In this, his last prophetic essay, Lawrence defines and presents the Dionysian as a dynamic "seeing through" the veil of the conventional, the forced pose, the "known," the empirical; in pre-Socratic Greece, for example, "'the cold,' 'the moist,' 'the hot,' 'the dry,' were things in themselves, realities, gods, *theoi*."³⁸ What is seen in the Dionysian perspective is a great flux of "life's" images, both agonized and beneficent, all filled not with materialist presence but with imaginative desire, with the "gods"—that is, with the "primordial delight" of imaginative consciousness. And in Lawrence's Nietzschean vision such creative delight exists in opposition to the "evasion" insisted on by the author of Revelations, with John's "proud impotence" so like the resentment and solace the Wagnerian listener is confronted with.

> By the very frenzy with which the Apocalypse destroys the sun and the stars, the world, . . . we can see how deeply the apocalyptists are yearning for the sun and the stars and the earth and the waters of the earth, for nobility and lordship and might, and scarlet and gold splendour, for passionate love, and a proper unison with men, apart from this sealing business. What man most passionately wants is his living wholeness and his living unison, not his own isolate salvation of his 'soul.' . . . We ought to dance with rapture that we should be alive and in the flesh, and part of the living, incarnate cosmos.[39]

The Dionysian is a means of ascertaining neither revenge nor false solace nor mechanistic truth. Rather it is the process of creating a world of yearned-for, imaginative truth, an earth whose soil is meaning, in which it is not only dirt but the stuff of significance into which one thrusts one's hands. Such are the images Lawrence offers in *Apocalypse*, as does Joyce in Stephen's epiphany at the end of chapter IV of *A Portrait of the Artist as a Young Man*.

What is the bearing of Dionysian dissonance on the rhetoric of such images in modern fiction? For the freed, creative, Dionysian consciousness, language becomes the scene, indeed the very process of tapping the capacity for imaging, for the metamorphosis of selves and of meanings. A result is the layering and complicating of modern narrative—its freeing from convention, its opening up to ambiguity. Language as dissonance formulates its images as freely created fictions. Particularly for the novelist with a consciousness of this fictiveness, language displaces its own self-destruction through its abundant waves of imaginative energy, the process of its dissonance. Finally, the "sinister resonance" of a work like Conrad's *Heart of Darkness* ("dwelling on the ear after the last note had been struck") is a metaphor imaging that freed critical and creative novelistic consciousness, above all, in the reader.

The "wisdom" resonating in dissonant fiction is particularly the awareness that, as modern fiction activates creative freedom *in the reader*, a profound risk is involved, which Lawrence and the novelists who play out the Nietzschean logic recognize. When Lawrence, for example, introduces the fertile image of Dionysis in his theoretical essays or of "Osiris cut to pieces" in his late *The Man Who Died*, the texts also simultaneously dramatize the potential despair in the object of Dionysian metamorphosis. Particularly, Lawrence's late fable takes up the notion, which Nietzsche also voices in *Zarathustra*,[40] of imagining for Jesus a final human trajectory, a full, agonized fall to sensuous earth. Resurrected, he is repelled by being worshipped by his followers, disappears to Egypt, and takes a Dionysian part there in the rite of a priestess of "Isis in Search" of dismembered Osiris.

> She was looking for fragments of the dead Osiris, dead and scattered asunder, dead, torn apart, and thrown in fragments over the wide world. . . . [S]he must gather him together and fold her arms around the re-assembled body till it became warm again, and roused to life, and could embrace her, and could fecundate her womb. . . . [S]he had not [yet] found the last reality, the final clue to him, that alone could bring him really back for her.[41]

The fleeing, alienated Jesus, she finds, is this realization of Osiris. In a prose of intentional uncontrol that characteristically forces together incantation and an exposing objectivity, Lawrence allows Jesus momentarily to know (both sexually and spiritually) his nakedness: "If I am naked enough for this contact, I have not died in vain."[42] Lawrence insists always here on the naked as the operative term and concept; his emphasis is above all on the vulnerable, the unmoored and stripped down, the fated transiency, the naked circling in death of Jesus. This metamorphosis in a continual death and stripping of former selves takes him out again at the fable's end, past Isis, navigating still further in death: "Let the boat carry me."[43]

Jesus in *The Man Who Died* experiences the risk and fate embodied in the image of Osiris—and of Dionysus and, indeed, of Orpheus—another dismembered god. This new, final, open-ended fable of Jesus contains precisely the challenge of dissonance to his hearer/reader, that the orphic song contains—and the same danger of dismembered, constantly disappearing and reassembling consciousness. An endless metamorphosis, charged with desire, in the midst of dying selves—Blanchot explains in "Orpheus' Gaze"—constitutes the knotted and paradoxical effect for the reader as for character and creator in twentieth-century narrative; "in his song . . . Orpheus is the dismembered, endlessly dying Orpheus his song has created. The song cannot do without desire and lost Eurydice and dismembered Orpheus."[44] The "song-text" which emerges for Lawrence and other modern novelists is composed of Dionysian dissonance. "Dissonance takes root in this nether region," Claude Lévesque concludes in "Language to the Limit," a region

> where resounds endlessly the mute scream let out by Dionysus. . . . Why be astonished that man, at the point of not being able to know and to bear it anymore, in appealing to the other, takes on the colossal and intolerable voice of the scream?[45]

In dissonant narrative, we hear—and see bared in the text and in ourselves—the potential despair in the object of Dionysian metamorphosis: It is the yearned-for release, both endless rupture and healing, compounded of the promise and the void of creative desire. These antinomies are best defined and understood through an examination of the crucial modern composer in the mode of dissonance, Arnold Schoenberg.

IV

The example of Schoenberg's music can further clarify the risks and opportunities for the perceiver in a musicalized text. In this composer's work, we hear a full, uncentering "roaring" of "unearthly" dissonance, to use images from the George poem sung in the finale of Schoenberg's second string quartet (1911); in that movement, as the strings violently disassemble a primitive scale of half-tones and the soprano offers a twelve tone melody as she sings of "breath[ing] the air of another planet," the listener hears a historic welcome of the free play of dissonance in music.[46] Indeed, the dissonance of this final movement of the 1911 quartet—not the serial controls of his later music—embodies the aesthetic of dissonance I explore and most clearly parallels the aims of modernist narrative. Schoenberg's dissonance achieves an intentionally difficult negation of music's grounding, commonly received, tonal conventions, a negation that becomes the only certainty left to assume (as Charles Rosen suggests).[47] Such dissonance—typical of Schoenberg's reimagining of the entire range of musical conventions—achieves its creative negation above all, as Rosen and Adorno indicate, *in the context* of the common musical language—that is, above all as opposition. Schoenberg drives to its logical conclusion the subversions propounded by the irony and ironic beauty of Mahler's symphonies; by Debussy's nuanced, synaesthetic, sometimes violent freeing of tonal centers from clichéd stability, even by Brahms, as he follows a Beethovenian logic of freed formal experiment, breaking atrophied lyric conventions in favor of developing a "musical prose," as Schoenberg suggests in *Style and Idea*.[48] The severe and radical logic in Schoenberg's music is an indication that—like Beethoven before him, only more "absolutely"—Schoenberg must attempt to explode the compulsively and falsely "affirming" stasis of the common language in order to emancipate the creative imaginative potentiality of language itself; both Rosen and Carl Dahlhaus emphasize that this "emancipation of the dissonance" is, as Dahlhaus writes, "the reason why tonality had been renounced."[49]

Schoenberg's aim is, then, to give his musical language the guise and substance of freedom, of a freed, continual becoming, shaped though it need be, by opposition and negativity. By exposing what Webern calls "the chasms in cliché,"[50] this difficult, disruptive, continual negation in the dissonant language becomes in part a protest against those too-easy, preformed, subjective affirmations to which the listener could otherwise surrender. Nietzsche's prescription for a dissonant aesthetic consciousness is fulfilled here, for—as Stanley Cavell points out—Schoenberg understood the dangerous necessity of dissonant composition: "that taste must be defeated," music "discomposed," in order to fulfill "the essential moral motive" of modern art.[51] Adorno describes this necessity in *Philosophy of Modern Music* when he analyzes what I am calling the Dionysian or dissonant consciousness in Schoenberg's music. The bourgeois illusion of individual subjective affirmation—the "illusion of authenticity"—is, Adorno writes, "sacrificed" because it is "incompatible with the state of that consciousness which has been driven so far towards individuation by the liberal order, to the point that this consciousness negates the order which had advanced it thus far."[52] Schoenberg's dissonant language presents that negation "as its goal. It is the surviving message of despair from the shipwrecked."[53]

Here we directly face the notion of the risk to the perceiver of dissonance. Schoenberg's listener is thrust into the activity of perceiving this new language of dissonance as a radical event in the language of consciousness itself. Its alienation and liberation of the "perceptual" process aims at straining the potentiality of tonality, of the order of consciousness and language exercised now in revolt at the outer limits of their capacity; the "fictive" creations of dissonance are radical particularly in that they demand an openness to negation in the listener. Schoenberg's self-consciousness about this demand on his diminished audience for the "new music" in Vienna helps to raise the issue of the performative impact of dissonance on the perceiver. By continually reenacting the "shipwreck" of modern consciousness (the casting out onto the waves of negation), the rhetorical strategy of Schoenberg's desperate negation leads the perceiver to engage a risk-taking, aesthetic and ethical challenge, one suggested by the antinomies which Adorno, Rosen, Dahlhaus, and others explore: that challenge is to encounter dissonant negation *as the form*, the language and activity ("not mere contemplation" as Adorno says in *Prisms*, "but praxis")[54] which embodies and achieves the survival of a freed consciousness in the modern period.

Jean-François Lyotard's critique of Schoenberg—in "Several Silences"—questions this freedom achieved by the composer's dissonant strategy (and his critique finds echoes in Jacques Attali's argument, in James Winn's contrasting of Schoenberg's "subjectivity" with Stravinsky's rhetoricity, and in certain criticisms of Adorno's "atonal philosophy" mounted, for example, by John Shepard et al.).[55] Lyotard would abjure what he sees as Schoenberg's puritanical seeking of "the tragic" and of a "therapeutics" in which music is a "discourse" of stigmatizing negativity and "control."[56] Instead, Lyotard would embrace an aesthetic of "circulation by chance," a "free wandering" suggested teasingly by images of Mao's noisy swimming in the Yangste and of Cage's play with noise and silence.[57] Yet where Lyotard hears in Schoenberg's dissonance a holding aloof from the free play of cultural sounds, there is as accurately a refusal to wrest apart—indeed an insistence on the link between—freedom and critical consciousness; and where he hears a "liquefying" or "dememorizing" of "domination" in Cagean play,[58] there coexists in such play also an ornamental, "aestheticized subjectivity" (as Dahlhaus suggests in *Schoenberg*), a postmodern forgetting and erasure—like plastic surgery—of the scars in twentieth-century history and culture, to use an image from Kroker and Cook's *The Postmodern Scene*.[59]

Schoenberg's art provides a revelatory model for modern fiction and particularly for its modernist aim: to prompt the perceiver first to imagine a disintegration of consciousness, a tearing apart of received, assumed "expressivity," a movement into contradiction, obliquity, parody, and silence, so that *Moses and Aaron* ends incomplete, fractured, its sung speech splintering into silence: "O word that I lack."[60] Yet, simultaneously, as the act of imagining can negate the processes of consciousness, Schoenberg's music offers a paradigmatic model for dissonant narrative which conveys within that negation a liberating attitude toward consciousness. Torn from the moribund habits of ordinary, habitual consciousness, the reader of the modern novel is challenged to engage the liberated fullness of fictive form within the suspension and negation of the habitual modes of perception. The "fullness" of alienation within the dissonant fiction of Proust, Mann, and Joyce achieves above all a full, imaginative, and critical freedom within the suspension of consciousness as a fiction—abundant, multifarious, playful, alien, and distressed.

5
The Dissonant Aesthetic in Continental Fiction: Proust, Music, and the Reader

I

Dissonance in twentieth-century fiction discloses an image of humanity in a shadowed, distorted state, rendered and judged as if against the hidden, remote horizon of its redemption. In dissonant narrative, the human being can become grotesque, a jungle ape or underground mole absurdly endowed with spiritual yearning, sensitivity and hope. Like Kafka's ape reporting to the academy, the dissonant voice of such a being addresses the modern reader and reports how the horizon of his world, once arching "as wide as the span of heaven over the earth, . . . [has now] narrowed and shrunk before me."[1] Kafka's "A Hunger Artist" presents another such being, and he can provide a point of departure for the study of dissonance in modern European fiction. The hunger artist is repelled by the ordinary sustenance of a shrunken life, by the packaged consumables all about. He laments the passing of starvation's appeal as a form of art, the most immaterial or antimaterial, analogous to the insubstantial art of music; its chic has become nonexistent next to the brutal materiality of the panther's art.

"A Hunger Artist" offers a provocative symbol for a European modernism which is simultaneously lofty in ambition and mired in carnival dust, a modernist art which is a powerful critique of bourgeois materialism, and yet is itself utterly insubstantial, a negation and distortion—certainly a negation of ordinary narrative. It is through his fabulous wrenching into parables of grimy deprivation that Kafka reveals, in Camus's words, "this hideous and upsetting world in which the very moles dare to hope."² The creature that represents Kafka's most famous worker in the modern workshop is Gregor Samsa, who dares to hope for nourishment, even in his hideous and disturbing condition. A source of such sustenance, he thinks, may be music. Of the family's food itself, he says: "I'm hungry enough, but not for that kind of food." But after the family's dinner, his sister plays the violin, perhaps to amuse their three cigar-chomping boarders, who harshly judge the apparent dissonance she produces. "And yet," Kafka writes,

> Gregor's sister was playing so beautifully. Her face leaned sideways, intently and sadly her eyes followed the notes of music. Gregor crawled a little farther forward and lowered his head to the ground so that it might be possible for his eyes to meet hers. Was he an animal, that music had such an effect upon him? He felt as if the way were opening before him to the unknown nourishment he craved.³

The musicalization of modern European fiction has been precisely the search for this "unknown nourishment he craved." Hermann Broch's *Death of Virgil,* in achieving a "polyphony," which ends "in a single great chord"—as George Steiner has observed, attempts "to transcend language towards more delicate and precise conveyances of meaning."⁴ The unknown nourishment he craved, indeed! Kafka's metaphor for music in "The Metamorphosis" suggests the features to be found in dissonant narrative; such fiction provides the reader, who is entrapped in the shrunken functioning of the modern world, with the possibility of an unknown, fictive sustenance. The distortion of such fiction enacts the negation of being in things but also its suspension in fiction, in a flux of possible metamorphoses, in a movement forever a step beyond the known, beyond entrapment as a thing, as bourgeois language and possession.

Proust's *Remembrance of Things Past* and Mann's *Doctor Faustus* take up this aesthetic of dissonance with its implicit ethic of reading, exerting pressure on us for an open, searching, critical, and self-implicating response. The role explicitly taken in their fictions by the music of Vinteuil and Leverkühn helps to clarify the workings of that aesthetic and ethic through a process of reperformance by which these novels' content echoes and enacts form and effect. Proust's and Mann's novels will be the focus of my discussion of European modernists, though Broch's brilliant novel is another classic musicalized narrative, and, of course, strong works by other novelists also aspire to the condition of music. In André Gide's *The Counterfeiters*, for example, the ambiguity of the author's own self-questioning is the most inclusive ambiguity of the novel and the signal feature of Gide's musicalization of fiction.[5] That subverting ambiguity—a melting together of form and content—focuses continually on the author's construction and deconstruction of *characters*. Albert Guerard rightly argues that Gide's concern with music is subordinate to the more character-oriented experiments in the author's project, is finally a "stylization" within Gide's involuted and spontaneous play, his antisubjective and antirealistic artifice, a display of subversive taste, intelligence, and sensibility.[60] There is a different reduction of the musical aesthetic and ethic to ornament and authorial gesture in Hesse's work, where, for example, the composer in *The Glass Bead Game* or Mozart in *Steppenwolf* is reduced to primal laughter and simplicity, indeed, becomes the mouthpiece of an authorial mysticism.[7] By contrast, the confrontation and empowerment not of the author but of the reader, constituting the deepest gamble of dissonant narrative, are to be found with much greater fullness and vitality in Proust's and Mann's fiction (and, in English, Joyce's fiction).

The similarities and differences among these novelists' uses of the terms and perspective of a musical, dissonant aesthetic are clarified when we note the seminal influence of Schopenhauer and Nietzsche on each novelist's vision. The ways in which the two writers take up, transform, and—in Mann's phrase[8]—"misuse" the two philosophers' aesthetics reveal both shared and opposed features of their imaginative practice. In this chapter, I turn to Proust, and in subsequent chapters, Mann and Joyce. Here let me first briefly sketch the pattern of the two philosophers' influence on the French novelist.

Proust attempts, as purely as possible, to embody a musical aesthetic in *Remembrance of Things Past*, and the combination of difficulty and achievement which results in his work illuminates both the reader's experience and the author's intention, profoundly influenced as it is by both Schopenhauer and Nietzsche. The role of music in Proust's novel is not only technical—a matter of the "contrapuntal" structure of leitmotifs or of a suggestive and ambiguous "musical" impressionism; nor is it only thematic, as in the central and illuminating role played by the fictive Vinteuil, his violin sonata and his septet—or by Wagner. Music's most significant place in Proust's work is to provide an aesthetic and ethic at the core of his vision. As we turn to Proust, and first to the philosophers' influences on him, my interest is less in examining the "musical" time or texture of the fiction, than to define the larger connections between Proust's central aims as a novelist and the reader's experience of his musically conceived art.

At the core of Proust's aim for fiction there lies a Schopenhauerian conception of the "purely musical impressions, limited in their extent, entirely original, and irreducible to any other kind . . . *sine materia*"—and so outside the all-encompassing manifestation of the Will in reality (I 227–28).[9] Proust's attempt to create fiction like music, for example like Vinteuil's music, attempts to achieve a Schopenhauerian vision of the breach between ideas on the one hand (that is, moments of spiritual illumination, self-less, redeeming, unwilled, and unconsciously attained by the autobiographical narrator) and—on the other hand—the vast and implacable spiritual corruption and death which are shown to unfold in human life. About the reader's relationship to this breach, however, he appears to be condemned to a characteristic failure in the face of the author's vision. Samuel Beckett suggests in his remarks on music and Proust that the reader's "impure" subjective perceptions of the narrative's musically conceived form inevitably distort and, Beckett implies, may "hideously" corrupt its "essential quality of ideal and invisible" transcendence.[10] (In this regard, Edmund Wilson's remark about Proust may be applied to the novelist's reader: envisioning an unbridgable gap between life and its transcendence through art, not only Proust, but his reader may be damned to "an eternal submergence in mud."[11]) The unintended and unexpected ambiguities which complicate the reader's relationship to Proust's effort to embody his high musical ideal in fiction will become clearer, first as I examine more closely the narrator Marcel's experience of the magical incidents of pure, unwilled vision, and then when I turn to the bearing on Proust of Nietzsche's insights into a musical aesthetic.

II

Proust's finest rendering of this aesthetic conception is to be found in *The Past Recaptured*, the final volume of *Remembrance of Things Past*. Here we encounter his overt assertion of the process by which—in Georges Piroué's view—reality is spiritualized through the process of the imagination; the birth of the spirit into temporal reality, Piroué suggests, is abortive, but born as the continual "becoming" of art's temporal, musicalized form, man's spirit lives in "la musique du devenir perpétuel."[12] In the novel's final volume, Proust's surrogate of unfolding self discusses the ideal function of his novel and of art generally—to reveal how the inner life might survive (through art and the artist's magical illumination of that life) in a time of individual and cultural disintegration. The narrator's initiation into "visionary" experience in this volume is the novel's climactic affirmation of the heretofore profoundly threatened existence of the artist's perception, a set of illuminations that sustains him and the novel he narrates. In the key scene of return to society after a barren isolation from it, the narrator Marcel is about to enter a Guermantes party when he experiences those intense, full, and exacting memories of past experiences, each time by means of an unwilled association of "involuntary memory" (as when the noise of hot water pipes magically revivifies his Balbec experiences). This mystical illumination is not a religious vision of God but a vision only of the inner life itself, for it exists in a world of the diminished and weakened spirit. It is a spontaneous vestige of man's mysterious inwardness.

Such illumination finds its model and precursor, as Marcel suggests, in the symbolic world envisioned by the music of Vinteuil, and in the last volume of the novel, the analogy becomes startlingly clear between musical symbols and Proust's sense of his fiction's form and aim—between the novel and particularly Schopenhauer's and the Symbolists' sense of music as a transcendent formulation of human time. This perception has been the shared basis for an understanding of Proust at least since Beckett's essay. Music for Proust is an enlivening "translation" of the reality of the artist's disintegrating inner life. Marcel's moments of vision provide him and the art he creates with a musically conceived symbolism, an oblique language "aux caractères figurés" which reveals the nature of the inner life in his time.[13] "The book whose hieroglyphs are patterns not traced by us is the only book that really belongs to us" (III 914). It is in this visionary and *figurative* sense that the artist's creation becomes simply a translation of the book of his inner being. To a degree far beyond what Marcel foresaw as his narrative progressed, the narrator's identity as an artist and man can indeed be associated with his aesthetic creation.

[T]he essential, the only true book, though in the ordinary sense of the word it does not have to be "invented" by a great writer—for it exists already in each of us—has to be translated by him. (III 926)

Ideally, the soul of the artist himself is transmuted and endures by means of this translation through involuntary memory and by means of its careful preservation in an elaborate, figure-laden prose that isolates and elevates in metaphor his vast luminous vision from the destructive darkness of reality and time's flow—that vision is thus "liberated from the contingencies of time, within a metaphor" (III 925).

The question this high and pessimistic aesthetic ideal makes the reader pose is, however, whether Proust's figures truly lift from time's flow the essence of each moment of human consciousness which, in its previous "real" existence, was obliterated by deadening falsity, disillusionment, and desperation. As Gilles Deleuze points out, the figurative action of metaphor itself is Proust's "analogue" to the effect of involuntary memory; each aims to be a means of formulating, preserving, and "not violat[ing]" the life of the past within the present.[14] The "internalized difference" between the past and the present (indeed, the present unfolding of the text) is a tension built into and reenacted by the process of what I would call Proust's musical imagination. Proust's central hope in this respect is focused on the redemptive power of a fiction modeled on Schopenhauer's and the Symbolists' conception of music.

This latter insight is the cornerstone of Jean-Jacques Nattiez's recent study of *Proust as Musician*. Nattiez argues that Proust yearned to follow Schopenhauer and the Wagner of *Parsifal* and the "Good Friday Spell" in creating an "absolute" musicalized text which can "arrest the wheel of time," thus solacing and redeeming writer and reader.[15] The complexity of Proust's work, however, cannot easily be reduced to the "disappointing . . . but human[izing]" debt to a single philosophical idea, or even to a "tour de force" revolving around Schopenhauer's static absolute.[16] Though for Nattiez the power of music in Proust is found in its quest for such an absolute, Piroué convincingly argues that music's power for the novelist is lodged in its continuously struggling and unfolding process, its upwelling of continual becoming. Proust's effort in this regard was to move his aesthetic beyond the influence and limits of Schopenhauer's and the Symbolists' idea of music as an ideal of transcendent and harmonious form. Indeed, the ambition and complexity of his novel are shaped also by Ruskin's, Bergson's, and Nietzsche's ideas. These latter stress that any absolute sense of being which art may embody is suspended in the fluid paradoxes of actual inner experience and outer human practice. The wheel of time cannot nostalgically be "arrested," but it can be reset in the spin of what Gerard Genette calls an "iterative temporality," attuned to the actual vagaries of time in which succession and duration are "subverted . . . perverted . . . and bewitched."[17]

Despite Proust's desperate and reverent hope that the musicalized time of his art transcends as it reimagines the contingent world which includes his readers, the encompassing aesthetic illusion in Proust remains by its very nature tied to the representation of imperfect reality. The admission of this tension, paradox, and the "imperfection" of the open-ended into his work impinges on and complicates the harmonious ideal; this is Proust's essential gamble, to locate the reader within the condition of fractured time, when each sequence is invaded by a simultaneity of image and analysis pouring through the waking dream of the text. The hope of such a strategy, I will later argue, becomes that the challenged reader will develop the moral and emotional "distinction" and "generosity" that Marcel identifies crucially with his mother and grandmother from the Overture onward (I 45). In the vivid twilit state into which reading is plunged, the disillusionments of experience are confronted. Its disjunctures are analyzed and their unlike features joined in paradoxical metaphors; a whore becomes an artist, a meal a church facade, and Marcel's favored servant Françoise—killing a chicken—becomes a preying insect (not to mention Charlus's later transformation in *The Cities on the Plain*). Similar associative insights become the pivot points around which massive transitions turn, and imaginative analysis grows, as in a dream, to inflate huge sentences and encompassing paragraphs.

In these ways, the novel's spiritual history of Proust's time and place strives to create the narrative equivalent not of what is a harmonious form, but of dissonance, and it does so in order to formulate the distorted yet surviving potentialities in man's spiritual life as they endure in experience. Finally and in part unwittingly, a Nietzschean conception of dissonance informs Proust's experiment with the symbolist musical aesthetic. Nietzsche's insight—that musical dissonance ultimately formulates the creative, Dionysian response of the perceiver in art—has a profound bearing here, as it does on the definition of modernism itself. For modernism asserts, among other things, a new partnership between the creator and the perceiver to wrest meaning from a disintegrating time and culture. The text of *À la recherche*—modeled as in this perspective it is on music—has the significance of dissonance as Nietzsche discerned it in *The Birth of Tragedy,* to formulate not a pure visionary fragment, not the voice of the author alone, but finally to formulate (to magnify, as Proust says) the response, in sorrow and awe and anger and compassion, of the reader herself. Given Proust's paradoxical vision of disillusionment, the reader's creative responsibility—as Nietzsche's idea of Dionysian dissonance suggests to us—becomes, to distinguish between the intention and the effect of Proust's use of the musical ideal, between the transcendent harmony of his aim and the assaulting dissonances of his creation.

The tension—between a reading which celebrates the aim of transcendence and a counterreading which emphasizes the text's ambiguities—calls into question the potentially false consolations and unities constituting Proust's apparent goal. (Gilles Deleuze offers an early poststructuralist parsing of this antinomy in *Proust and Signs;* for a later deconstructive version, see Paul de Man's analysis in *Allegories of Reading.*)[18] The tension between inimicable readings (rooted as they partly are in opposed aesthetics of harmony and dissonance, of Schopenhauer and Nietzsche) promises to demonstrate—through that very tension, mutual alienation, or discord—how reading itself might endure, how writing and reading remain possible, how meaning yet unfolds in modernity. The tension between the two Proustian readings indicates and embodies the understanding of the dissonant imagination, for dissonance is the musical form of both the disappearance and the unstable struggle of meaning to endure in art.

III

I turn now to the vital place in Marcel's inner world of Vinteuil and his music, for they yield an ambiguous revelation—what Proust intended to be an affirmation—of the nature of the novel's form and aim. When Marcel first presents Vinteuil in *Swann's Way*, the composer is burdened by an inherited and nervously puritanical bourgeois identity. As Marcel sees, his lesbian daughter is an essential cause of his tortured ill-ease. (The tension between artistic creativity and "corrupt" experience is the crucial theme broached here.) Vinteuil's attitude toward his own music is so modest that, seemingly a strict puritan, he is too embarrassed to play it for Marcel's mother. That his music should reveal a magical inner world or beautifully illuminate an ideal world of the Combray that Marcel himself idealizes seems unlikely to the narrator because he observes that Vinteuil seems imprisoned by his familial pain, by his pathetic Combray identity.

The secret world hidden in the composer's soul is obscured by a real world of personal and social wills demanding his submission, by an oppressive reality in which Marcel plays an ambiguous part. On the one hand, Marcel clearly responds to the magic and spiritual illumination of a reality which is generally menacing to him, an illumination he experiences at moments in his Combray life—for example, before the steeples at Martinville. On the other hand, Marcel cannot help but become enmeshed in the external world of experience, of willful desire and disintegrating expectations. This ambiguity informs Marcel's entire narrative, and its imprint marks the evocation of the sonata, Marcel's and our first entry into the world of Vinteuil's music.

Marcel first introduces us to the sonata through Swann, a character whose experience occupies an important part of the world of spiritual possibility that Marcel's narrative envisions. Swann becomes a gigantic presence in the narrative, and his "way" becomes a mythic path along which both narrator and reader journey, through the stages of increasingly profound aesthetic and, indeed, musical epiphanies. In the first volume which bears the name of this journey, Swann is in love with Odette and, to be with her, he attends Mme Verdurin's salon, where he hears Vinteuil's sonata. He responds deeply and unexpectedly to one phrase of it, and has Odette play it often on the piano. That phrase becomes for him the key to and expression of an ideally beautiful inner world. Swann is, however, a disappointed idealist, disappointed first in his love for Odette and, moreover, morally bankrupt in his experience as a dilettante of art, patronized by corrupt aristocrats and, as a Jew, assimilated to an anti-Semitic world. A dissatisfied inhabitant of the world of the will and the failed spirit, he desperately and unsuccessfully *uses* Vinteuil's phrase as a sign for his and Odette's disintegrating love affair. The tension between the two aspects of his identity—his involvement in both an ideal and a real world—is suggested by the metaphors used to describe his response to the sonata, the metaphor of a fleeting, romantic moment of longing for a woman seen for a moment passing by, or the metaphor of a quasi-religious quest, "to consecrate his life" (I 230), a quest fairly soon forgotten. Swann's desperate aestheticizing of experience is thus tested and ironically exposed by the novel. Indeed, Swann's own irony, which says neither yes nor no to snobs and social castes, is extended implacably to include creativity and aesthetic experience, and this irony exposes a like unreliability in both social identity and the imaginative process.

The irony here with regard to music is that it leads not merely to the revelation of the inner life; it becomes a "recreative" instrument for the use of a desperate and deadened soul. The novel's own obsession with sorrowful impotence before corrupt reality is suggested by the extended presentation of Swann and, finally, by the fact that Swann uses Vinteuil's music to indulge his sorrow at the failure of his experience and to attempt to will an escape from it. In Swann's "use" of the sonata, a deathly shadow is cast over its description because its forms contain the particular light of Swann's soul. It is, thus, appropriate that the sonata is described as a dark blue sea at night, over which the pallid light of the moon shines. The music has become the flickering, immaterial transformation of the emotion of Swann's inner experience into an expressive form, both ideal and consoling.

The vision Marcel presents of the meaning of Vinteuil's music is further developed when Swann encounters the sonata again after the sorrowful apparent disintegration of his affair with Odette. The music makes vivid the past moments of his intimate and vain sorrow and turns his thoughts to Vinteuil's own suffering. The musical phrases recreating such moments in their emotional lives are themselves the inhabitants of a mysterious, dreamlike, and supernatural world. Here is the final and essential part of Marcel's analysis of Swann's second encounter with the sonata:

> Vinteuil's phrase, like some theme, say, from *Tristan*, which represents to us also a certain emotional accretion, had espoused our mortal state, had endued a vesture of humanity that was peculiarly affecting. Its destiny was linked to the future, to the reality of the human soul, of which it was one of the most special and distinctive ornaments. Perhaps it is not-being that is

the true state, and all our dream of life is inexistent; but, if so, we feel that these phrases of music, these conceptions which exist in relation to our dream, must be nothing either. We shall perish, but we have as hostages these divine captives who will follow and share our fate. And death in their company is somehow less bitter, less inglorious, perhaps even less probable. (1381)

Music's higher reality for man, it appears, is the result of its acquisition of sentiment, its accretion of human feeling and the human soul. Paradoxically, however, the quotation also asserts that, if one sees experience itself as unreal, nonbeing, then the immaterial form of music is a sort of reality, destroyed only if the human soul dies, a captured spiritual reality opposed to the death which seems to be experience. The fragile, wishful extremity of the sense of music's value Marcel evokes here is, finally, an expression not only of the ambiguous self-indulgence of Swann in bitter sorrow, but also of the ambiguities in Proust's enthused yet defensive idealization of music. What Walter Benjamin calls Proust's "paralyzing explosive will to happiness"—his joyous yearning for transcendence through fiction-making—is, thus, complicated by the falsifying, Schopenhauerian invitation that Benjamin sees Proust simultaneously offering his readers: "to view his *oeuvre* . . . from the time tested, comfortable perspective of resignation, heroism, asceticism."[19]

The narrator's mention above of Wagner's *Tristan und Isolde* helps define the nature of Proust's ambiguous idealization of music. With its vision of art's relationship to the experience particularly of the sexual world, Proust's novel attempts—like the project of the Symbolists—to complete the work of Wagner. Like Proust's vast novel, this opera is huge in scale and is dramatically ordered by the experimental use of leitmotifs; most importantly, *Tristan* purports to embody Schopenhauer's philosophy and particularly his view of sexuality. In *Tristan*, sex is linked to the exhaustion and death of society's hold over Isolde and Tristan, and this link underlies also Eliot's Wagnerian echoes in "The Waste Land" as well as Proust's invocation of the composer. A darkened version of Wagner's vision, Proust's novel appears to assert that only outside of experience, in nonbeing and a musically conceived art, can man's spirit find true and full expression, that ideal consummation toward which sexual passion in particular, and the Will in general strive without success.

Proustian narrative—in its frenzy of Dionysian analysis—does not Parsifal's luminous and mythic stop time, nor Siegfried's invention of a cultural myth on the verge of time's end, of Gotterdammerung; rather, Proust's fiction celebrates Tristan's temporal decay, the distorted potentialities within time's cycle, its ceaseless process. Even Nattiez, with his favoring of the Schopenhauerian reduction and the Parsifal model, acknowledges that music "is inscribed in time . . . [and] is a process"[20]—though he finally follows the early structuralist, mythic model of narrative, folk or modernist or both, as "a machine for eliminating time."[21] The process of Proust's work, a dialectic negotiating the juncture between the ideal and its decay, is pervaded by a narrative subversion, or to use Gennete's word in a new context, a narrative "perversion."[22] This paradox in the novel offers an example of what I would call thematic or spiritual dissonance: Aesthetic responsiveness—Swann's, Marcel's, the reader's—is simultaneously celebrated and questioned by the narrative in a ceaseless discord.

This alienating effect, this dissonance, applies beyond Swann's experience of music to much of Marcel's narration, for example in the suggestively ambiguous connection drawn between sexual and spiritual pursuits. Marcel's desperate need for the ideal illumination of art subtly echoes his dependence on the women and men he idealizes; the pattern is felt even in the beginning of the novel, tapping our compassion and enshrining Marcel's "mystical" response to the madeleine's taste, the "overture" with Marcel's self-consciously visionary illumination of his Combray home and of the child Marcel awaiting his mother's goodnight kiss. When he approaches adolescence, his impulse is to idealize the girl he lusts for—Gilberte. Finally, in the climactic relationship to Albertine, Marcel's sexuality—as one pursuit of a spiritual ideal—becomes a desperate and deadly battle; from his first troubled glimpse of Albertine through her captivity, Marcel places demands on her which become the untempered weapons in a fight waged between his spiritual aspirations and the fluid and corruptible reality in which he invests emotion and spirit. This emotional investment destroys and is destroyed by Albertine, perverse and unknowable.

Marcel's sexual life is, then, a failed experiment and expression of his spirit; in the knotted sexual world which he inhabits with Proust, art becomes the only successful embodiment of his spirit (this only after a long purgatory). As his love affair with Albertine degenerates, Marcel significantly encounters Vinteuil's septet, and we will see that the encounter further reveals the ambiguous connection which the novel formulates between art and experience. Finally, the life and music of Vinteuil, and Marcel's life out of which emerges his vision, are alike in that both reveal the "profound union between genius (talent too and even virtue) and the sheath of vices in which . . . it is so frequently contained" (III 265–6). In regard to music alone, the surrounding world—the sheath—of vice is embodied by the sexual inversion of Vinteuil's daughter, of Albertine and her friend (the devoted sole transcriber of the great septet), and of the music's violinist perfomer, Morel. In part through Morel, sexual extremity helps to destroy Marcel's aristocratic friends, Saint-Loup and M. de Charlus, whom Proust makes into the deadened yet rare and peculiarly brilliant "aesthetic" emanation of an already dying and corrupt culture, so that the Guermantes Way and finally each strand of plot and theme in the narrative becomes riddled with alienation and ambiguity, with negating paradox, with dissonance.

IV

One ambiguity, then, in the idealization of music here is that it is in part defensive. A pure and transcendent musical art becomes, in Proust's desperate vision, the undistorted recipient of the great emotional dependence and spiritual investment which experience grotesquely distorts and defeats. This paradox is fully as much embodied by the novel's experimental form as by its engagement of explicitly musical subjects. For one pivotal example in *The Captive*, the idealized relationship of Vinteuil's music to the world of human disintegration in which it is embedded, and out of which it arises, is ambiguously asserted in Marcel's key description of the septet as it impinges on him in the midst of the complex chaos of posturing at a Verdurin party. Unlike the pallid sonata of Swann's experience, the septet is described by the metaphor of a new world illuminated as though by the rising sun; in it, Marcel sees a rose aurora of daybreak and hears "a mystical cock-crow" (III 252). The world Vinteuil's soul inhabits here, is the country "unknown . . . [and] forgotten" of the individual life.

> [T]he art of a Vinteuil . . . exteriorizes . . . the composition of those worlds which we call individuals and which, without the aid of art, we should never know. (III 258–59)

The septet exteriorizes, or rather reveals ("fait apparaître") the soul of the same Vinteuil who lived in Marcel's bourgeois Combray, itself containing the seeds both of art's visionary life and of spiritual death. The fact that his soul endures, in the septet, triumphs over the human negation which, however, paradoxically surrounds it. In its triumph, like all music, its mysteriously expressive forms take one into the center of its vision of inwardness and enable one to attempt to perceive the existence of one's own inner life, or at least the possibility of its existence. The septet is a mirror in which Marcel sees the form of, the possibility of envisioning, a true inner life, and it is a mirror in which he can make out some of those luminous impressions of his own which become cornerstones of his final vision and the novel— "foundation-stones for the construction of a true life: the impression I had felt at the sight of the steeples of Martinville, or of a line of trees near Balbec" (III 262–63).

Yet, just as the edifice Proust erects on those cornerstones is marked by ambiguity, so, too, is Vinteuil's septet for, behind the ideal revelation of the music is a desperate and embattled intensity which Marcel himself suggests characterizes its sensuous forms. This post-Franckian music, by magnifying emotion (to use the Proustian phrase), is like his novel with its unique combination of desperate intensity and ideal vision. With its extended analyses and evocations, Proust's ideally magic illumination ends by magnifying the temporal and emotional existence of every moment of experience, and as the novel's final sentence celebrates, it makes of Marcel and each major character impinging on his consciousness "géants plongés dans les années" [giants plunged into the years]. These gigantic characters never cease being creatures of paradox, the flux of their ambiguity ever decaying and reforming, sensuously slipping beyond the grasp of one's yearning for transcendence, even as their ambiguity is an emblem of their potential for transcendence.

Proust's characters become in part like Rilke's giant angels, greater than any towering architecture of awe which material hands might build: "Like an outstretched arm / is my call," Rilke writes in his Seventh Duino Elegy, as his art struggles to imagine, let alone to encompass, the always paradoxical "Ungraspable one, far above."[23] The angel of that elegy, measurable only through paradox and negation, is linked to the ambiguity and audacity of Proust's musical ideal, the musicalized constructions of his overarching central characters. As I study the characters and the other structures constituting his musicalized narrative, my interest is in examining the limits and ambiguity in his idealization of music. Proust's narrative dissonance, proclaiming those limits and that ambiguity, is, as we saw, thematic, but it is also stylistic and rhetorical, infusing every aspect of narrative form. The ambiguity of the novel's formal experiment parallels and reflects that of the novel's theme revealing the use of music as a desperate and defensive escape from the failure and corruption of experience.

The same ambiguous defensiveness and enervated frustration can characterize Proust's formal, stylistic effort to capture and spectacularly to heighten the expressiveness of every moment and gesture in experiences which, in their temporal existence, imprison and corrupt the human spirit. The thematic example of the Baron de Charlus's sexuality, revealed in the first twenty-three pages of *Cities of the Plain*, is, for instance, simultaneously an example of rhetorical dissonance (II 623–56). A wash of analysis suspends his and Jupien's sexual behavior in a fluid continuum, replete with insect and vegetable analogies, historical references, and subtle psychological penetration. The effect of this analytical flux is the effect of dissonance. In this hip turned, or that double entendre uttered, the "Dionysian" flux of narrative dissonance reveals and affirms in the midst of "inversion" and inexorable decay the continuum of multiple, exfoliating, atomized possibilities for meaning in sexual experience, all conceived in the frame and unfolding of fiction.

Another example of such dissonance in form as well as theme is the heightened evocation of the adolescent Marcel's first meeting with idealized Bergotte, in *Within a Budding Grove*. The passage begins with the sentence, "The name Bergotte made me start, like the sound of a revolver fired at me point blank" (I 589). The paragraphs following that sentence confront the "youngish, uncouth, thickset and myopic" human figure who materializes in Marcel's sight amid the pistol's smoke, and these pages constitute a fascinating essay on the humanity and genius of the paradoxical figure of Bergotte, an essay full of brilliant literary effects, of metaphors that—no matter how subversively prosaic (like the revolver's shot)—are a self-consciously elaborate, paradoxical "temple" designed "to enshrine" at least the complex reactions of Marcel both as an adolescent and as a mature narrator. Those pages are full of an intensely literary self-illumination which (though not the very language of the inner life, an obscure darkness illuminated and seemingly liberated) is finally a suggestive, radically extended, and dissonant artifice, attempting to juxtapose and to accommodate the narrator's naive yet characteristic disillusionment with the social and moral reality of lived experience.

The conception of narrative dissonance—rhetorical and thematic—which I broach is not concerned with a musical prose depicting musical experiences, nor is it concerned purely with the analogy (developed in different ways by Piroué, Nattiez, and Scher) between, for example, Wagner's gigantic musical structures and Proust's temporal experiments. Primarily, my concern is rather with the bearing of dissonance on the aesthetic and ethical aims of his novel. The implacable paradox of Proust's dissonance is that his musically conceived fiction becomes both a defense against and a searching, risky testament to negating, impermanent, alienated reality. To the extent that this clash of goals is self-deceptive, his novel might draw a criticism like Nietzsche's of Wagner (a criticism ironically paralleling that which Beckett, in his admiring study of Proust, makes of opera in general): that such art's inflation of form and its spectacular and visionary heightening of disillusioned experience are the self-indulgent expressions of impotence and despair. The challenge of the novel is for the reader to maintain the awareness that it is above all through the drama of alienation that the process of meaning and transcendence is activated in all its Proustian fullness and vitality.

This is the central paradox of the novel—that the work is the moving, magnified, and brilliantly analytical vision of the progressive disillusionment of the narrator and author, of the defeat of Marcel's spiritual expectations centered on certain personalities, certain beloved women, certain works of art, and finally a visionary form of memory (which like the promise and figure of art endures, sustaining and undefeated). This "vision" of blindness, of a disillusionment bearing the repeatedly defeated aspirations of Marcel's spirit, endures in the novel as an inverted and defensive entity, as an obsessively self-conscious and analytical force which continually asserts its own distorted survival in the prose of the novel. This brilliant, analytical prose roots much of the narrative in the inescapable and disintegrating world of a "real," corrupted, and even deathly prosaic personality and society. Seen in this perspective, Proust creates the narrator's ambiguous literary mask of evocative and analytical prose which enshrines an illumination and analysis of each moment of the experience of a life and a society, yet it is a sometimes defensive and self-indulgent mask which attempts to protect the narrator from the failure, certainly, of reality but also of the artist's inner life. This mask threatens as it protects the narrator's perception and humanity, and it reveals the discordant ambiguity of Proust's effort to create a language like that of music, expressive of, and finally achieving the continued survival of his spirit.

V

To define the reader's relationship to Marcel's ambiguous narration and to Proust's aim for his musicalized narrative, I want first to describe Proust's conception of the role and form of perception he requires of his reader. In the again partly Schopenauerian and Symbolist view that Proust develops, music (with its exacting and suggestive forms and the obliquity of their expressive content) contains no subject but the inner life itself, no mediating mask to justify or to deaden the listener's contemplative relationship to those forms. Ideally the listener becomes, in novelistic terms, the hero of music's revelation of the inner life, because its forms live only in the listener's contemplation of them, and they become the forms of the listener's perception of his emotional and spiritual world. As a result, musical form depends on the listener—with the potential depth of his perception and humanity—to discover himself in the work; it places his inner life at the center of "vision." This conception is the model for both Proust's use of form and his expectations of his readers. "I would furnish them with the means of reading what lay inside themselves" (III 1089). His ideal purpose is to provide a symbolic language, like music, both enabling and requiring the reader to explore and discover the forms of his own inner life.

Yet the terms of Proust's visionary language for the survival of the inner life are the experience and identity of an *artist*, as continual witness absorbing into self the encompassing spectre of character and milieu. The reader encounters a vision of spiritual survival which is also the radically extended, yet in a sense traditional, autobiographical fiction and mask of Proust's own existence and development as an artist. The latter ideally becomes a symbol for the former. The reader's role, however, remains ambiguous. On the one hand, he is the conventional novel's observer, as through a window, of a vast vision of the development of the artist in his world, a vision which, like any window, is subject to the inauthenticity of being dressed; on the other hand, the painstakingly created and profound musical form Proust conceives of here aims to offer a compelling formulation of, a mirror for, the reader's own potential spirit, his inner experience. Proust wanted to achieve the latter, to place the reader in the position of the artist, at the center of the work, reading "his own self" (III 949). The author's effort, then, becomes to provide a sort of "optical instrument" that enables the reader to see "what, without this book, he would not have perceived in himself." The narrator continues:

> [T]he recognition by the reader in his own self of what the book says is the proof of its veracity, the contrary also being true, at least to a certain extent, for the difference between the two texts may sometimes be imputed less to the author than to the reader. (III 949)

The final words on the difference between the two texts are still another indication of the defensive, self-isolating ambiguity of Proust's actual rather than ideal expectations of his reader. Proust's work "has as its center a loneliness which pulls the world down into its vortex," Walter Benjamin writes of the text's ambiguous impact on the reader; "Proust's pointing finger is unequaled. But there is another gesture in amicable togetherness, in conversation: physical contact. To no one is this gesture more alien than to Proust. He cannot touch his reader either; he could not do so for anything in the world. . . . This is what Fernandez has formulated so well: 'Depth, or, rather, intensity is always on his side, never on that of his partner.'"[24]

The reader wonders, amid the simultaneous vision and disillusion at the end of the novel, if its phrases and scenes are not the expression of the narrator's unacknowledged doubt of the power and value of his own illumination—as if that illumination were also a self-serving mask to hide a profound and corrupt emptiness in the artist's soul, or as if his vision and prose did not provide the language itself of the soul, but instead merely dissected the monstrous corpse of a defunct form which contained a vacant, deadly spiritual silence. When we encounter the moving and violent transition from the narrator's contemplation of his vision to the Guermantes party with its reunion of the dying, the ambiguities of the novel strike us most forcefully; for the ironic and insightful sense of human waste in the scene seems a more powerful expression of the narrator's tortured nature than the preceding assertion of the value and power of visionary illumination.

Illusion or illumination? Such paradoxes challenge the reader to become the active listener/reader Nietzsche calls for and, for example, Ernst Bloch and Theodor Adorno describe. Challenged to develop beyond the defensive limits of the narrative, Proust's reader is called on to develop the creative, multiple sense of self which more profoundly underlies the narrative, to develop the sense that "the self therefore has the freedom of being the variety of its disguises" (to use Leo Bersani's characterization).[25] Finally, the reader is invited to combine an imaginative responsiveness with a moral penetration and generosity akin to that of Marcel's mother from whom Marcel yet defensively hides his own imaginative fluctuation of self; in this way, we must break continually beyond the narrator's limitations. The reader must take up the mantle, which Adorno sees Proust carrying naively, perhaps defensively, yet masterfully: the mantle of a readerly engagement of art, in which aesthetic experiences "become [subjective], an element of . . . consciousness."[26]

> Proust's subjectivism looks to art for the . . . salvation of the living. In opposition to culture and through culture, he represents negativity, criticism, the spontaneous act that is not content with mere existence.[26]

The reader must engage a vision far more ambiguous and complex than Proust's own conception of form and of the reader's role suggests. Proust would enable his readers to encounter without ambiguity the book of themselves in *À la recherche*; he would make his novel, like music, a formulation of the depth and complexity of their inner lives. Yet, musical form, in truly mirroring the modern spirit, reveals the distortions of that spirit even as it endures them; thus, the beauty of musical form in our time has itself become distorted and "dissonant," a fact that Nietzsche was the first to recognize. Though music has been, for the West, the ideal formulation of the inner life and, indeed, because it is so, modern music reveals to us the imperfect shape which the inner life takes in the twentieth century; in this regard, Nietzsche's effort was to alert us to the modernity of dissonant form and to its challenge to the reader that he place himself at the creative and evaluative center of the form and its ceaseless and disintegrating flux of meaning.

In Proust's view, however, the transcendent beauty of a musical form remains the unmaimed spiritual survivor of the murderous and perverse accident which is reality and time; the reader seeks in vain there for the irony and indeed the distressed humor of a recognition of how the beauty of art itself is attenuated as it endures in our century. The disparity I note between Proust's ideal intention and his actual, more complicated achievement is the result of his desperate, defensive use of a musical art which, he asserts, transcends all use and time. Experiencing Proust's vision paradoxically darkened by a lack of consciousness of its deepest nature, the reader must rise to the creative task of sustaining, on his own, an insight at the dissonant center of the fiction. We must supply our own dangerous, purgative recognition of the enduring insight that Nietzsche describes as the Dionysian response which dissonance evokes from us, a paradoxical perception embodied differently in each of the major modernists' novels. Not only the artist's experience, but also his vision of transcendence, are distorted and spiritually attenuated by the nature of modern life. The dissonances themselves become the narrative's signs of meaning, the "divine captives who ... share our fate."

6
The Ethic of Dissonance: A Study of Mann's *Doctor Faustus*

A rending, inspired pressure is exerted, as we have seen, on the reader of Proust. His *À la recherche* instills and requires a richly ironic but not perjorative recognition of the disparity between the luminous intentions and the darkened world-rendering experience the novel holds for us. The deepening significance of such an ambiguity becomes apparent when we direct our attention from Proust to Mann and particularly to *Doctor Faustus*. Here again music is central as both subject and experimental model, and again the aesthetic of dissonance enables us to locate the audacious irony, the spiritual risk, and finally the ethic of reading at work in the novel.

I

It is helpful initially to survey the several contexts—biographical, musical, philosophical, and literary—in which Mann's tragic masterwork develops. Paradox is the signal feature of Mann's life and work, and it is no accident that he turns to dissonance as an aesthetic model for the treatment of his essential themes. Even the family into which he was born is marked by contradictions. His father was a distinguished and wealthy yet failing Burgher; his mother artistic, unconventional, of German-Brazillian origin; and the brother of this cultured, "nonpolitical," German youth was a brilliant, challenging leftist, who accompanied him on his inevitable, life-revealing sojourn to Italy at twenty-one. When at twenty-five he published *Buddenbrooks*, a powerfully orchestrated generational chronicle exposing the decay of a Burgher family, he was received and embraced by precisely such distinguished families in Munich and, indeed, married the gifted, part Jewish daughter of such a family. Each of the ensuing landmarks in his work is marked by such ironic juxtapositions between traditional culture and its disintegration—the novella *Death in Venice*, for example, and the apologia of self and culture in *Reflections of a Non-Political Man*; these works are not unrelated to Faulkner's efforts both to confront the tragic recognition of cultural failure and historic guilt in the South and to testify to the possibilities of ongoing life there. After revealing such paradox writ large across the face of European culture in *The Magic Mountain,* and after receiving that culture's highest prize, the Nobel, for his efforts, Mann turned to the Jewish bibilical narrative of the Joseph novels just as Nazism rose to power in Germany; the tetralogy's art, and not only its occasion, is marked by similar paradox, by the fusion of cultural myth with fictive playfulness in both character and narration. Finally, with the move to California during the Second World War, Mann wrote *Doctor Faustus* while part of the expatriate community, itself an ironic and paradoxical experience.

The musical novel he wrote in Pacific Palisades is shaped by profound discontinuities in the perspective of this tourist of culture's ruins, lodged now on the quaking edge of the brave new world. Holding on with him were an extraordinary assemblage of expatriates—above all Schoenberg, Stravinsky, and Theodor Adorno, a new guide to "the new music." Music became the key metaphor and fictive testtube for the novelist's imagination of the implacable paradoxes through which he and his times lived. *Doctor Faustus* resonates with the history of music itself, and with the ideas I explored in my earlier discussions of Beethoven and Schoenberg. The innovations of other composers, too, are essential to an understanding of Adrian Leverkühn's compositions in the novel. For example, Mahler—whose widow, Alma, circled too about Los Angeles—responds with travesty and mourning to the early modernist situation of art. A model for Aschenbach as well, Mahler confronts the eternal silence sensed after the death of Wagner, whose "last words"—according to Mann, like Ibsen's, in drama:

> [are] apocalyptic climaxes, majestic in their sclerotic languor, in the mechanical rigour of their technique, their general tone of reviewing life and casting up accounts, their self-quotation, their flavour of dissolution.[1]

The Ethic of Dissonance 81

This description begins also to characterize Mahler's musical language. His symphonies complicate Wagnerian chromaticism to the point of an almost fully freed dissonance which marks his travesties of folk themes, his desperate quotation of children songs—all filled with the pain of finding in each form nothing but cliché yet simultaneously insisting still on expression, on the possibility of meaning. Massive climaxes give way to silence and then to primoridial gestures of creativity, yearning for expression in the face of the apocalyptic end of all the bloated clichés and dead content of culture.

The alternative to Mahler's symphonic gigantism in early modern musical culture is a minimalism which he himself practices in his startling shifts to chamberlike effects at moments in the symphonies. Debussy was the great practitioner of such effects, complicating harmony and fragmenting melody and sonority into increasingly essential associative gestures, so that expressive meaning becomes a process of associative fluidity, confronting the listener with sudden, sinuous shifts from the langorous to violence and back. Debussy's synaesthesia—like Baudelaire's—insinuates into musical experience the external world of the sea's flood, the firework's burst; in this way, the open-ended music juxtaposes the banality of the "real" with the infinitely nuanced world of the "imaginary." The inbuilt irony—like the effect of dissonance—confronts and calls to Debussy's listener for engaged judgment. Debussy's irony becomes the prod, finally, for Adrian Leverkühn's first composition in *Doctor Faustus*, "Ocean Lights," which pushes Debussyan irony into alienated and alienating parody (151–52).

The composer who drove Debussy's logic to its assaulting conclusion, into a rhetoric beyond even what Mahler conceives, is Stravinsky. His appropriations of folk and "neoclassic" banalities yield parody and a dissonant hallowing, which travesties the lyrical centeredness of expression unavailable to modern culture. His ballet scores transform Debussy's fluid strategy and harmony into a new means to shock the bourgeois listeners of 1913 into reaction, rather than self-reflection, for Stravinsky's sinuous melismas and assaultive syncopations would initiate the listener into a fictive world in which the actual violences of sexual, personal, social, and political experience seem at play and at risk. Stravinsky's ballet scores are positioned at the point of confrontation between two opposed, modernist goals or ideologies, and the debate over which is his deepest allegiance affected Mann as he was writing *Doctor Faustus*. One view asserts that the ballets seem to embody "a corporeal imagination": the fullness of their sensual upwellings and violences bestow the illusion of objective authenticity on "the whole dancing body," as Roger Shattuck describes the fertile, destabilized world of sensation with which Stavinsky assaults the listener.[2]

An opposed view is offered by Mann's friend in the forties, Adorno, whose ideas influenced the composition of *Doctor Faustus*. He writes that Stravinsky's embrace of the sensual dance emerges from his nostalgia for the lyrical ideal of authentic expression which has disintegrated in our time, but on which his objective, rhythmic, and corporeal sensuousness yet insists. Stravinsky's music is, according to Adorno, an "authoritarian" deception which falsely "advertises its authenticity as something which it has already attained."[3] The phantoms of the authentic and the objective can become instruments of totalizing control in a world where "reality's" forms, and the clichés enclosing sensation need the continual testing of a freed, critical consciousness. Autonomous authenticity or critical freedom? Stravinsky's "poetics of music," for all his ironic skepticism about both art and life, proclaim the objectivity and autonomy of aesthetic form, and place him squarely in that modernist tradition which favors the time-less "authenticity" of transcendence over the "critically" engaged process of a temporal, self-questioning, dissonant art.

Yet the greatness of Stravinsky is partly that he does not abjure the confrontative aesthetic of dissonance, just as Schoenberg does not completely exclude the sensuousness of the dance and its implicit aesthetic. The best works of each achieve a different, tense meld of the two traditions of modernism. Schoenberg's struggle to create a new musical language is one of the subjects in chapter 4 of this book, and here suffice it to note a few salient points about his music. He confronts head on that issue—of music's impact on the listener—which is embedded in the irony, travesty, and assault of the composers I have discussed above. Of them, Schoenberg was the most sensitive and self-critical about the problem of how meaning is achieved in modern music. In order to keep engaged the unnumbed consciousness of the listener, his music attacks all sentimentality and cliché, all consonance confirming the solace and timeless stasis of the transcendent. Adorno writes that the composer "sacrifices the illusion of authenticity, viewing it as incompatible" with the freed, critical, dissonant process by which our consciousness brings meaning into existence.[4] "All music purports a becoming," he continues—that is a *process* and not a static state or autonomous object.

Adorno's conception has a decisive bearing on Mann's vision in his late novel, and it is worth noting that the novelist's turning to Adorno—in 1943, in Los Angeles—for help with *Doctor Faustus* was a choice consistent with that vision. Not only was much in Adorno's thought illuminating for the novel's conception of modern music as well as of Beethoven (as Carl Dahlhaus and particularly Gunilla Bergsten document),[5] but Adorno himself is a figure linked to the key characters of Mann's novel, Leverkühn and above all Zeitblom. Mann's pages in *The Story of a Novel* on Adorno, the "tragically brilliant" German-Jewish refugee "operating on the highest level,"[6] evoke Adorno's profound self-scrutiny in the midst of the confusions and disasters of modernity, a penetration and integrity that link him to fictive embodiments of damaged, disappearing humanism like Zeitblom and Leverkühn, or even Joyce's Bloom and Stephen. Adorno's insights pertain precisely to the struggle and affirmation of alienated, illusory "humanness" envisioned by modern novelists as well as by the composer Schoenberg and indeed the fictive composer Leverkühn. The link of Schoenberg to Mann's rendering of Leverkühn's struggle for meaning in music has been the subject of several critical discussions and a few brilliant exegeses like Dahlhaus's essay on the paradoxes of "fictive twelve-tone music" for Mann and Adorno.

Mann's distress at Schoenberg's resentment for being implicated in the portrait of Leverkühn marks how profoundly attuned the novelist is to the achievement of the real composer (see Bergsten's study as well as the exchange of letters reproduced in the appendix of Patrick Carnegy's work).[7] That achievement includes the invention of serial technique but, most important, exceeds it. Schoenberg did not rest content merely with an intellectually objectifying technique. His best scores did not depend on "pure" serialism—for example certain preserial works like the opus 11 piano pieces or the Second String Quartet, and later the tragic, serial ferocity of the String Trio or the grand and terrible ambition of *Moses und Aron*, with its eclectic form. In such music, he wanted the listener to engage the dissonant expressivity and significance of his composition in the spirit of searching freedom.

Schoenberg also uses his essays as a means to convey his desire to avoid the totalizing grip of objective, autonomous, transcendent form on the listener. In "About Music Criticism," he discusses the difficulty of realizing Schopenhauer's aesthetic in the new music which must confront the worn-out "language of the world" and must combat the tendency of music's solace and "wisdom" to become a pat, glib "reduction."[8] The simultaneous attraction to and movement beyond Schopenhauer is a recurrent fate for the writers I consider—Nietzsche, certainly, as well as Proust and Mann. Both Schoenberg and Mann avow the influence of Schopenhauer's vision of music as the "Idea" itself, outside the Will's irrational encompassing of reality, leaving an unbridgeable gap between tumultuous reality and music's static spirituality. Yet each also transmutes and reforms this musical ideal through the Nietzschean strategy of using a language of unstable, ambiguous, and ironic dissonance, critically activating the reader and sensitizing him to the possibility of reduction, of a "life-denying" passivity in the listener/reader's experience of art.[9]

Once more, here, let me briefly note Nietzsche's conception of dissonance—for, beyond its illumination of Schoenberg's form and impact on the reader, it is a crucial part of Mann's many-faceted use of Nietzsche in *Doctor Faustus*. At the center of Nietzsche's conception is the insight that the harmonious forms of traditional art and of civilized order are not able to contain the ceaseless, dialectical struggle between spiritual yearning and disillusionment—that is, the dissonant struggle to endure modernity's disorder in consciousness and in fiction making itself. Mann's reader experiences not the vast and paradoxically static, timeless oasis which is Schopenhauer's and in part the Symbolists' conception of music, he experiences an often devestating, yet also protean and tragicomic temporal structure where irony and ambiguity reach out to assault and activate the reader's perception.

Significantly, the difference between Mann's essays on Nietzsche and his fictive applications of Nietzsche is precisely that distinction between nonfiction's "symbolic" assertions of *timeless* truth, even in irony itself, and fiction's "allegorical" incitement of the reader continually to search *through time* for meaning. This partly Derridean distinction extends from Stanley Corngold's discussion of Mann "as a reader of Nietzsche"; he writes that Mann never reads the philosopher "except to discover in him a rhetoric for affirming attractively his own position,"[10] shifting—as Mann's circumstances change—from "irritated mimesis," to humanistic appropriation, to censure.[11]

Corngold's key question, about how self-serving Mann's readings of Nietzsche seem, is answered implicitly by the essay's brief, final comments on *Doctor Faustus* as a rendering of "the general phases of a *Bildung*"—that is, by Corngold's appreciation of the shifting, *fictive* growth of the novel's images of Nietzsche, from "Imitation" through "Commemoration."[12] This appreciation of Mann's use of Nietzsche's ideas *in fiction* helps now to point my discussion, too, toward its proper goal, an analysis of dissonance in Mann's novels. For it is in the novels' brilliant challenge to the reader to activate his critical engagement that we find Mann's deepest motive—in dissonant fiction, if not in his essays—for shifting between opposed applications and interpretations of Nietzschean irony:

> between Nietzsche's irony as pervasive, as informing even life with a play of perspectives and fictions punctuated by the will; and . . . Nietzsche's irony, on the other hand, as the smiling self-betrayal of the ironic intelligence, whether from love for the German bourgeois or the search for personal integrity through renunciation.[13]

Beyond "the art of reading Nietzsche,"[14] Mann is "a master" of fiction that instructs us in the Nietzschean art of reading.

II

The shifting, destabilizing gradations of Mann's irony are a crucial means by which he achieves his dissonant narrative's reliance on the reader's vital and difficult engagement. Experimental, pervasive, ironic discord is the source of the impact of two of his greatest works, *Death in Venice* and *The Magic Mountain*. Irony in these works is not the instrument and occasion for a luxurious aestheticism but for accepting the paradox of a life in disintegration; it is a means of controlling the collision of terms in that paradox, allowing and accepting the coexistence of life and death, beauty and collapse, growth and decay. Irony—with parody—is a creative play for Mann, the worth of which depends on the potential, human value of the life or term it calls into question. Finally, ironic dissonance becomes the malleable, shifting instrument for melding and balancing such paradoxes into a promise—always unstable and in process—of wholeness in the self, in its becoming.

The affirmative potential of this ironic process is profoundly tested by Mann's 1911 novella. In *Death in Venice*, Mann uses a severely controlled and highly integrated prose in order to envision the spiritual disintegration of Gustav Aschenbach, a great fictive European writer of Mann's own stature—indicating the doubled irony of self-implication. With assiduous care, the narrative prose adjusts itself to each stage of Aschenbach's collapse. Mann formally enacts the paradox of the work's content by stretching the ironic structure to the point of self-destruction, yet as a brilliant artwork, it denies that very assertion of disintegration. Such ironies infuse the narrative's every turn, from the very start. Aschenbach himself, for example, uses a beautiful style to proclaim an austere asceticism. As well, the high, classical Greek aesthetic he values celebrates the subversively androgenous, erotic, and aristocratic beauty he now glimpses. The narrator's own controlled, subversive, and hence, again, doubly ironic comment is that

> in almost every artist nature is inborn a wanton and treacherous proneness to side with the beauty that breaks hearts, to single out aristocratic pretensions and pay them homage.[15]

As Aschenbach's absorption with Tadzio progresses, the narrator's prose resonates with increasingly destabilizing, dissonant ironies: the aging artist contemplates the youth's tie to breakdown and decay, noting his small physical imperfections, and Aschenbach "did not try to account for the pleasure the idea gave him."[16] Indeed, pervasively, he is not conscious of his projection of his own narcissistic self-absorption everywhere, so that, for example, one grotesque transition links his welcome of love for the boy to the clichéd image of dawn as the naked god of the sun arisen.[17] The corruption and death of both art and life in modernity require irony to keep alive the possibility of an engaged consciousness, yet near the end, sitting in the piazza of his squalor, the Master "had outgrown the ironic pose."[18]

At one point toward the end, Mann unrelentingly intensifies the ambiguity of the work to its most extreme point when he allows harsh and jagged Dionysian rhythms to impinge upon his narrator's severely ironic, Apollonian prose for a still unflinching paragraph in order to render the extremity and animallike degradation of Aschenbach's dream. Here Mann's irony, accommodating spiritual extremes and confronting the reader with the task of insight and judgment, is given a most discordant and challenging expression:

> Foam dripped from the lips [of the savage rout], they drive each other on with lewd gesturings and beckoning hands. They laughed, they howled, they thrust their pointed staves into each other's flesh and licked the blood as it ran down. But now the dreamer was in them and of them, the stranger god was his own....
>
> The unhappy man woke from this dream shattered, unhinged, powerless in the demon's grip.[19]

Assaulting and exploring the reader's own sense of spiritual possibility, the ironic form here intermingles the voice of brilliant aesthetic detachment and control with the voicing of the Dionysian and distorted struggle of Aschenbach's now disintegrating spirit. As the reader is forced to engage "the whole cultural structure of a lifetime [as it is] trampled on, ravaged, and destroyed," the reader is also made to see that the irony of Mann's dissonant form confronts the reader with the responsibility to endure the degradation at the center of Mann's own vision and form, at the center finally of modernity's highest spiritual struggles. In the final lines of *Death in Venice*, we are left with the recognition, challenging, and potentially subverting our sense both of the self and of civilization, that the nightmarish "immensity of richest expectations" possessing Aschenbach's last moments declares the possibility of the death of the spirit and of a culture.[20]

The modern fate of Western culture is an underlying subject of Mann's fiction generally. In part, his work forms a vision of the disintegration of that culture—its thought, its humanity, its art (particularly music), and its political and social relations. Mann's vision of that fate is, as we have seen, a complex, ironically ambiguous, and dissonant form. His vision engages a disintegrating world in order to achieve what affirmation is possible, and, as a result, Mann's dissonant art engages the risk that he erects ruins rather than self-sustaining spiritual forms. *The Magic Mountain* embodies exactly that risk, and its great edifice—a symbolic summation of European culture immediately before World War I—is a most brilliant and enduring experiment in the musically conceived manipulation and enrichment of fiction's temporal structure, with its heightening and foreshortening of the passage of time, its subtly enlivening and complex use of leitmotifs, and its continual play with stated and unstated antitheses, its dialectical irony which is Mann's version of Nietzschean dissonance. Our concern is to define a specific and vital aspect of that irony, its informing relationship to the reader's role and experience.

Mann's irony is what he follows Goethe in calling a "serious jest."[21] It is an extended and seriously playful version of the apocalyptic irony in *Death in Venice*; a crucial feature of *The Magic Mountain*, its irony shapes the novel's effort symbolically to suggest and contain the structure of modern European culture. Again like the earlier novella, the work is profoundly self-conscious—here about its own overfull narrative voice, its obsession with the reader, its structural manipulations of increasingly hastening time, and its parody of the Bildüngsroman in which now a diseased and hermetic withdrawal becomes the path of whatever growth is possible in modernity. Like dissonance as Nietzsche conceives of it, the novel's self-conscious ironies challenge the reader to accommodate and to explore the extremities that the structure of experience is revealed to contain, extremities of heightened vision and spiritual corruption and of the spirit's death as one pole of existence. Mann's audacity here is to confront the reader with so much ironic rendering of the sheer, teetering edifice of Western culture, and he does so, above all, out of a controlled desperation, to provoke the reader into grappling fully with the question of how to survive in the face of the overweening contradictions.

Unraveling the ironic web of the novel's complex temporal form, the reader recognizes his ironically conceived, struggling, and imperfect surrogate in the hero of the novel, Hans Castorp. The "heightened, stock-taking" spirit of the main character is, of course, irretrievably caught in that ironic web which both weaves and captures a vision of his changing inward experience of seven years at House Berghof, his experience of physical and spiritual health and disintegration—of Clavdia, of Peeperkorn, of Settembrini and Naphta. Thus caught up and made finally to meet his fate in the carnage of the first World War, Hans Castorp is, as the narrator finally says, "more than we thought," for he is not only the focus of the novel's ironic revelation of a spiritual world, but also himself takes the Nietzschean risk of engaging that world and of seeking those insights that the reader too seeks and which range beyond the dialectic of Settembrini's and Naptha's reductions.[22]

The heightening of Hans Castorp's perceptions culminates in his own vision, in the chapter "Snow," which renders and accommodates the spiritual extremes of an Apollonian ideal and its negation. He thus comprehends and explores the potential for disintegration and death at the center of the life of the spirit. The Nietzschean extremes of his inner experience are also clear when, near the end of the novel, he himself is the perceiver of an apparent "fullness of harmony"—that is, of recorded music from the new acquisition of the House, the phonograph which obsesses him. Mann's irony, of course, locates in Hans Castorp's response to music the same ambiguous matrix of spiritual vitality and disintegration that underlies the novel's entire vision, a fullness not of harmonious but of dissonant revelation, which gives the reader his responsibility for judgment and self-exploration. Hans Castorp, listening, is himself taking up a similar responsibility. He thus presents us with our flawed and imperfect double, the reader's partial surrogate whose response to a Schubert song, though a travesty of Nietzsche's prophetic sense of the need for self-overcoming before the fate of European culture, yet engages the profound Nietzschean contradictions enlivening music and the "dissonant" form of *The Magic Mountain* itself. For Hans, the resonant beauty of "The Lime Tree" stirs both a "spiritual sympathy with death" and an inner call for "self-conquest."[23]

> [These] prophetic half-thoughts . . . soared higher than his understanding. . . . One need have no more genius, only much more talent, than the author of the *"Lindenbaum,"* to be such an artist of soul-enchantment as should give to the song a giant volume by which it should subjugate the world. Kingdoms might be founded upon it, earthly, all-too-earthly kingdoms, solid, "progressive," not at all nostalgic—in which the song degenerated to a piece of gramophone music played by electricity. But its faithful son might still be he who consumed his life in self-conquest, and died, on his lips the new word of love which as yet he knew not how to speak. Ah, it was worth dying for, the enchanting lied! . . . These, then, were Hans Castorp's favourite records.[24]

Here and throughout the darkening climax of the novel, the shrill jest of Mann's irony is a means of accepting the risk implicit in the contradictions of Hans's response to music: that a musical art simultaneously embodies the possibility of transcendent, redeeming beauty and the devastating, distorted expression of man's tragic and disillusioned desire to transform reality. In the middle of "The Lime Tree,"

Hans's beloved eternal time gives way to the stormy search through ironically complex, ongoing time: This is the stumbling yet life-giving path of the human. Such pervasive and challenging humor in Mann's discordant irony both forces and enables the reader to confront and endure that inextricable contradiction by exploring how it implicates and reveals his own sense of spiritual possibility in a disintegrating world.

Here, also, is a central distinction between Mann's and Proust's visions. Proust attempts to assert the possibility in fiction of a pure, symbolist transcendence, of a vast and will-less Schopenhauerian stasis in art's illumination of experience. Yet Proust's ideal becomes, in his formation of the reader's actual engagement, a fluid, striving and imperfect experimental form whose discordances challenge us to recognize the ambiguity of Proust's ideal in its realization; that ambiguity of Proust's partly Wagnerian form constitutes its dissonance.

Mann and Proust share a concern both with music and with the genesis of the artist's vision, and the novels of both use a musical aesthetic to envision the disintegration of Europe's social and cultural order in the twentieth century. In *Doctor Faustus*, a novel written decades after *The Magic Mountain*, Mann again, like Proust, explores the connection of those themes to the power of music to reveal the nature of modern man's experience. Yet, Mann's novel of a modern composer's life, with its labyrinthine irony, offers a more concerted and self-conscious dissonance. Instead of yearning for the artist's ambiguous capacity to illuminate a totally darkened world, Mann applies to the possibility of such illumination a constant and subverting irony which leaves his reader with a sense of the redeeming power not of the visionary or the celebrant, but of the searching, critical, and free human consciousness. We turn now to the connection between Mann's novel and the modernist ethic for fiction which I am exploring and which a dissonant aesthetic helps to define. That ethic makes fiction's meaning depend, in a newly vital sense, on the reader's creative engagement as he confronts the disintegrating ambiguities and distortions of modern, dissonant narrative. This reliance on the reader constitutes the ethic of dissonance I explore also in the fiction of Proust, Joyce, Conrad, and Lawrence. It is in the light of such an ethic that the significance becomes clear of Mann's effort in *Doctor Faustus* to explore the relevance of a musical aesthetic to the survival of fiction in the twentieth century.

The Ethic of Dissonance

III

Written at the time of World War II, *Doctor Faustus* is the novelist's greatest experiment in musically conceived form. Here again the conceptions of dissonance and a musical paradigm for fiction help us to explore the informing aim and meaning of modern fiction—that is, to understand how we read modern fiction. In addition, dissonance has become the subject of *Doctor Faustus* as well as the aesthetic model for the fiction. Mann's own discordant form voices the spiritual disintegration underlying and crippling the narrator Serenus Zeitblom's humanistic biography of Adrian Leverkühn, who is himself the Faustian and Nietzschean composer of modern, dissonant music.

To a degree far beyond the playful and steadily unfolding ironic dialectic of *The Magic Mountain*, the dissonant character of Mann's musically conceived form here puts its radically subverting and finally tragic mark on the aesthetic surface of the novel, on its contrapuntal time scheme, its symbolic structure of parallels and leitmotifs, and its richly involuted prose. A central example of the novel's leitmotifs is the recurrence of the name Esmeralda as a butterfly, a prostitute, and a musical motif—each time beautiful but deadly, and stirring Leverkühn to laughter as a child, to risk as a young man, and to excoriating lamentation as a composer (15, 154–55, 486–89).

In the larger, structure of the novel, every novelistic element has a subverting echo in another. For example, in the center of the novel (chapter 16 through 25), the sexual, musical, and spiritual discoveries are counterpointed with their corollary disintegrations: Leverkühn's sexual encounter with Esmeralda and the choice to contract syphilis, his embrace of parody and then of "serial" control as the chosen musical means of expressing the chaos of self and time, and finally his spiritual discovery and wager with a self-reflexive, parodistic devil in order to consolidate his powers in hopes that anguish will yield creative depth.

After this dense counterpoint, the seeds of demonic risk yield the grotesque and tragic ironies of the novel's second half, connecting Nazi and artist, perverse violence and bourgeois life, a time of world carnage and a time of artistic creation, passion and spirituality, madness and intellect. At novel's end, the costs are played out in the death of Leverkühn's Echo and in the agony of the *Lamentations*. Throughout these developments, the narrator strives to build sensitive, honest, yet homaging images of Leverkühn and his spiritual milieu, but

Mann's own parodistic irony simultaneously makes a travesty of the narrator's effort by having Zeitblom unwittingly reveal the madness and corruption of the world Leverkühn inhabits—for example, of impotent or possessed characters like the pitiful violinist Rudi Schwerdtfeger, the desperate and driven Inez Rodde, or the menacing Dr. Breisacher.

It is Adrian Leverkühn himself, Mann's Faustian composer, who reveals most overtly the nature of the novel's dissonance, of both its Nietzschean and its musical foundation. In *The Story of a Novel*, Mann acknowledges that Nietzsche is a detailed and profound model for Leverkühn's experience; and there is the note appended to the novel itself, indicating that Schoenberg is the model for the description of Leverkühn's serial technique. (Schoenberg's episode of anger with Mann, in part for not at first explicitly acknowledging his model, is only one of the many suggestive and assaulting ironies surrounding the novel.)

Clearly Nietzsche's conception of dissonance is vitally relevant to the significance of the dissonant music inspired by Leverkühn's abstractly willed experience of evil. Both by recognizing his spiritual disintegration and by creating radically dissonant music, Leverkühn—in Nietzschean terms applicable also to Schoenberg and beyond—wills the risk of disillusionment and despair as he subverts already dying spiritual and artistic conventions. "The goal of Nietzsche's desperate strategy," Erich Heller writes in his eloquent and seminal reading of the novel, "is to insist on the Mephistophelean prospect and yet not to despair, and yet to glorify, indeed to transfigure existence."[25]

In Mann's vision of Leverkühn's similar, Faustian strategy, each spiritual affirmation Leverkühn attempts, no matter how transfigured or aloof, finds an implacable connection to an element of inhuman negation. I noted a key example of that connection in the relationship between Leverkühn's inspired, intellectually brilliant music and his self-willed, self-destructive affair with the syphilitic prostitute Esmeralda. Modeled on an incident from Nietzsche's biography, this is an abstractly pursued passion which leads to his syphilis and to a diabolical self-destruction, yet it simultaneously enables him to create brilliant art. Even as it fulfills a hellish "compulsion," it is experienced as a struggle to endure that very compulsion, to find shelter even within the hellish fate, even to love; at least Zeitblom imagines the possibility that the lovers' coupling is "an act—if the word be permitted me—of love" (155). Later I will turn more fully to the role of Zeitblom's struggling affirmations in the drama of narration here, which is finally a drama of reading, of Leverkühn's primary and most heroic reader/listener.

Leverkühn's pact with his devil—who offers spiritual corruption and death in the guise of artistic genius—is not only the hallucinated embodiment of the inhuman and abstract evil occupying and torturing his soul; it is also the chillingly ambiguous, conflicted expression of Mann's vision of the disintegration of European culture in this century. Leverkühn's meeting with an insinuating devil, whose language is the corruption of an archaic dialect, reveals the potential for corruption at the center of the modern creative spirit. The fascination and terror charging Mann's ironic rendering of Leverkühn's Nietzschean and Faustian strategy—"to make the All sing," but now in a fullness of dissonance—suggests the relevance of the composer's music to the struggle in Mann's own work to endure the spiritual collapse in the modern period.

Leverkühn's music is composed at the end of the disintegrating tradition of European and specifically German music and in a spiritually corrupt age. The music is marked by grotesque, ambiguous parody—ambiguous because it both derisively subverts yet subtly depends on the creative tradition of the past. "Everywhere is Adrian Leverkühn great in making the unlike the like," Zeitblom writes (378). Here, parody joined with travesty constitutes the universal maelstrom of "Apocalypsis" in which opposites are concertedly joined, simultaneously empty, yet still horrifyingly expressive: aestheticism yields barbarism; consonance, hellishness; dissonance, loftiness; children's voices, the devil's laughter; and the eerie beauty of glissandi becomes the emblem of destruction. Leverkühn's music becomes a sort of hypercompression of all the modernist musical subversions—beyond Debussy and Mahler, beyond even Stravinsky and Schoenberg, on the edge between modern and postmodern. Nevertheless, even as this extremity of parody is a destructive technique, like dissonance, it is part of the desperate, Nietzschean strategy. It takes on the risk of revealing the dark and diminished nature of the modern spirit while, at the same time, it suggests the paradoxical possibility of a negative spiritual transcendence. This becomes clear in the composer's final work, the *Lamentations of Doctor Faustus*, which is in part a parody of

Beethoven's Ninth Symphony with its "Ode to Joy." Leverkühn's work

> is, as it were, the reverse of the "Ode to Joy," the negative, equally a work of genius, of that transition of the symphony into vocal jubilation. It is the revocation. . . . But it is not only that [this "Ode to Sorrow"] more than once formally negates the symphony; . . . no, for even in the religious it is negative—by which I do not at all mean it denies the religious. (489–90)

For Leverkühn, man's spirit—the "religious"—survives in this century but now diabolical and in despair. The composer is compelled to parody the Ninth because he is obsessed by the fate, the dying of man's spirit just as he is compelled equally to assert its now darkened, attenuated, yet continued existence. A ferocity of destructiveness is matched by a plentitude of creative power and need, in which the terrible necessity of destruction becomes an index of the modern negated fate of the human, the image or "fiction" of the human, in the years between 1914 and 1944.

Syphilitic, and his diabolical pact fulfilled, Leverkühn goes mad after the completion of his work, and dies; he is unable to heed its "light in the night." Yet the work's origin is a profound self-recognition in the face of the death of the nephew Leverkühn loved: it is the composer's "yea-saying to his being unredeemable. An utmost virtuosity comes together with an utmost authenticity," as Heller suggests.[26] The profoundest ambiguity, however, of the hope in his last work is not only that it cannot affect the soul from which it has arisen, nor that it exists in silent clarity and the abstraction of memory, but that finally it only exists in Serenus Zeitblom's humane vision, in his prose which both masks and embodies the greater "music" of Mann's complex work. Leverkühn himself, however, is denied such a hope. His very attempt to achieve it is ambiguous and negative because it is relentlessly and destructively willed, so abstractly "spiritual." Abstract will makes his meeting with the devil and the terrible, pitiful death of his nephew Echo, seem cold-blooded, the vacant yet tragic expressions of an abstractly schematic and willed fate. Leverkühn's humanity is exhausted by the quality of austere abstraction, of intellectual purity, characterizing his commitment to art and to evil. Spiritual abstraction itself becomes the devil's tool, and, finally, the composer's attempt to create a new dissonant music expressive of modern man's inner life is so abstract as to be hellishly inhuman, even as it may be the sole spur for spiritual survival here. And the novel links this corruption of spirituality to the corruption and violence of Germany's fate and indeed of Europe's modern culture.

IV

When Leverkühn subverts classical forms and uses their essential qualities of abstract balance and purity to envision the spirituality of his soul, classical purity ends up masking spiritual corruption. How does Mann's own art relate to its vision of Leverkühn's music? And what is the connection of his art to his emphasis on the evil shadowing Leverkühn's music? In a characteristic answer offered by the last generation of critical studies, Erich Heller argues in *The Ironic German* that Mann's imaginative purpose is to create a "moral protest . . . against [art's] new freedom that so easily deteriorates into 'libertinage,' cynicism, and irresponsible playfulness, or—as . . . revealed by the Adrian Leverkühn of *Doctor Faustus*—to an alliance with the very powers of evil."[27] Paradoxically, however, Mann's vision (as Heller elsewhere suggests) also illustrates the inevitability of that freedom and its peculiar and dangerous fertility.

In another insightful study, well representing the current generation of critical response to *Doctor Faustus*, Susan Scaff defines that fertile, critical freedom as the capacity and, indeed, "responsibility to appropriate timeless myth to the cause of history"—that is, to narrate and to judge historical temporality and specifically the fate of the modern.[28] She employs Kermode's demythologizing of apocalyptic fiction in *The Sense of an Ending* as an instrument both to define Leverkühn's efforts before the *Lamentations* to escape into apocalyptic myth, and to critique the tendency of Mann's critics to escape the novel's pressure on the reader by focusing on technical, aestheticizing, indeed harmonizing perspectives.

Finally, it is dissonance itself—as I have argued—which can become a mechanism of freed, critically aware movement within and beyond "the apocalyptic trap" Scaff identifies.[29] In the midst of the terror of cultural disintegration, Mann's reader is confronted with the challenge of dissonant irony and ambiguity as the pervasive elements of the novel's form; such are the signal qualities of its experimentation with a musical aesthetic. The dissonant novelistic language

Mann creates is the form which can render and place modern man's consciousness at the darkening center of vision.

The abstract and pervasive irony of the novel seems to have at times the negating force of Leverkühn's own humanly exhausted music, and the irony of its "metaphysical" drama reveals a dark and diabolical spiritual underground out of which modern art and culture appear to grow. The novel is a vision of the battle, the confrontation, of the death of art with the commitment to art, and the risk of its irony is that it seems alternately a protest of and a capitulation to the dying of the modern spirit. This central paradox is the subject in the novel of Kretchmar's lecture on Beethoven's last piano sonata, opus 111. The lecture is an early occasion for Leverkühn's recognition of the tie between a culture's music and barbarism's irrational voice (59). With a desperate stutter, Kretchmar says:

> Beethoven's art had overgrown itself, risen out of the habitable regions of tradition . . . into spheres of the entirely and utterly and nothing-but personal—an ego painfully isolated in the absolute. . . . [Here] the subjective and the conventional form a new relationship, conditioned by death. . . . Where greatness and death come together, he declared, there arises an objectivity tending to the conventional, which in its majesty leaves the most domineering subjectivity far behind. . . . The sonata had come, in the second enormous movement, to an end, an end without return. And when he said "the sonata," he meant . . . the sonata in general, as a species, as traditional artform. . . . Opus 111 was the farewell of the sonata form. (52–56)

In a sense Mann's novel is also an opus 111, only far less serene, its majesty bleak and self-destructive. With its abstract and enduring irony, its objectivity tending toward the parody of convention, its subversive revelations of the sources of artistic inspiration, and also its sympathetic but profoundly weak narrator—*Doctor Faustus* is the farewell not only of the novel form as it had existed but of the possibility for traditional European art.

What we have called the strategy of dissonance in the novel is not simply Mann's liberated expression of "an alliance with the powers of evil," like Leverkühn's music with its desperate wager for transcendent stakes. In its ultimate effect it is like Schoenberg's music, as I have attempted to describe it. Mann here achieves a paradoxical affirmation; this novel about dying art and death in life yet tacitly and desperately affirms—as a novel—the embattled existence of a sensibility and intellect committed to the continued life of European art, even as a purely fictive potentiality. The irony at the center of this "terminal" work is, according to Heller, a way of "giving a traditional form to the very experience of its disintegration, of desperately resisting despair"; it is an outgrowth of "the particular character of Mann's moral intelligence. . . of a moral spontaneously resolved to preserve the continuity of form as a symbol and promise of something absolute and indestructable."[30] "Absolute and indestructable" is, however, a somewhat optimistic description of the "form" and promise embodied by Mann's ironic art. His evasive and tortured irony makes the novel's form as dangerous and subtle as a labyrinth and as bleak and fragmented (intentionally and carefully so) as a ruin. His work, thus, is the promise of something absolute in the ways that a labyrinth and ruin suggest the absolute—or, using Nietzschean terms, in the way that dissonance suggests the distorting extremity of modern man's struggle for transcendence. The moral and spiritual promise held, indeed barely sustained, by such a paradoxical form is diminished, if not even "deformed." Irony in Mann becomes not merely a recognition of the gap between "fantastic" reality and the abstract perfection of art; it is the process by which even a most attenuated spiritual affirmation can endure.

V

In its confrontation of art with the death of art, what larger affirmation can the dissonant irony of the novel's form sustain? Any affirmation here is asserted by the novel's narrator, by Serenus Zeitblom, Leverkühn's biographer, whose mind and prose are a lens through which we view the composer. Finally, I want now to examine how the reader's role is implicated in the ambiguities, the now more-than-serious jest, of Mann's rendering not only of the novel's "hero" but of the narrator himself. From the start of the novel, the sympathetic, "academic" voice of the narrator seems unwittingly sinister and, indeed, a parody of an intellect's faltering hesitation before the apparently insane events which Zeitblom describes and before which he is powerless. Our narrator is a classical philologist (again a sort of Nietzsche) who is paradoxically writing the humanistic biography of a composer and friend at the time of the Nazis in Germany. He is held helpless in the thrall of a splintering time, of the clash of times he duly reports—1912 or 1918 or 1929, and his present 1943–45, and then implicitly his address to our readerly, fin-de-siècle present in the 1990s. His commitment to humanism in the midst of time's collapse, his torturously evasive and apologetic narrative, the combined sympathy and apprehension (the awe and fear) he feels for his brilliant friend all express an ambiguous tension between Zeitblom's inner values and his experience of the forces that destroy them, forces he finally sees both in society and within the human spirit he values. Mann makes the ambiguous tension that Zeitblom voices—that is, the dissonance of the narrative—assault the reader's own humanity with the terror of its contradictions. Manipulating the fading voice of Zeitblom's crippled and baffled spirit, Mann is suggesting how the human spirit may survive by means of an ironic awareness of such contradictions, an acceptance of divided, fragmented experience. As William Honsa suggests, like parody "the device of the narrator is another means of getting at those realities of faith and feeling which are the source of artistic vitality."[31]

It is, thus, appropriate that Zeitblom's struggling appreciation of the *Lamentations* offers us the perception of a symbolic hope arising, an obscure and diminished phoenix, from the ruin of modern European culture; here at the climax of the work, Zeitblom haltingly evokes the "mourning" and "despair" in the music yet paradoxically yearns even as he hesitates to speak of the possibility of "consolation" and "transfiguration" in the *Lamentations*.

> [G]rant that expressiveness—expression as lament—is the issue of the whole construction: then may we not parallel with it another, a religious one, and say too (though only in the lowest whisper) that out of the sheerly irremediable hope might germinate? It would be but a hope beyond hopelessness, the transcendence of despair—not betrayal to her, but the miracle that passes belief. For listen to the end, listen with me; one group of instruments after another retires, and what remains, as the work fades on the air, is the high G of a cello, the last word, the last fainting silence, and night. But that tone which only the spirit hearkens, and which was the voice of mourning, is so no more. It changes its meaning; it abides as a light in the night. (491)

As the reader comprehends the meaning of this music for the composer's spirit, it is, in a sense, a relief to be reading Zeitblom's prose, its expression of a humane and ironic attitude toward the spiritual darkness surrounding him. Zeitblom seems to retain at least an echo of his humanity and sensitivity even as his perceptions are unwittingly confused and relentlessly twisted by Mann's dark and parodistic vision. The novel itself closes in a manner not unlike the *Lamentations;* Zeitblom's voice is here the lamenting "high G of a cello" which, when its humanity is silenced, yet abides transformed into "a light in the night," into the hope for humanity that however exists only in the silently activated memory of the reader—for Zeitblom's faltering spirit is distorted and overcome by the weight of ambiguity and terror that Mann's form enables the reader alone to bear.

> When out of uttermost hopelessness—a miracle beyond the power of belief—will the light of hope dawn? A lonely man folds his hands and speaks: "God be merciful to thy soul, my friend, my Fatherland!" (510)

With that prayerful voicing of three words whose contents have become grotesquely stripped of humanity, the meaning becomes clear of the ironic sympathy the novel yet sustains in us for Zeitblom even when he seems the travesty of a narrator, impotent before the fates of his friend and nation. Floated on the sea of Leverkühn's—and Mann's—artifice of irony, parody, and so of suspended, vanishing meaning is the menaced, contingent *possibility of meaning* within Zeitblom's narrative, precisely *within* its ironic suspension and vanishing. The dim and vulnerable light Zeitblom symbolizes is the light of the human which barely endures the darkness of modern man's spirit, intellectually powerful but, to Mann, profoundly corruptible, its humanity practically destroyed.

The fact remains of Zeitblom's vulnerability and impotence before the many-edged irony and the complex onslaught of the vision he is made to engage. At the end, the meaning—the obscure hope amid hopelessness—that the novel unfolds is that only the reader is placed in a position to survive the vision of disintegration, that in other words she alone is in a position, vulnerable and contingent as it is, to use both intellect and humanity in perceiving and enduring a vision of the battle of art and man's spirit with their negation. Not Zeitblom's wishful, emptied voice but Mann's fully discordant form enables the reader to confront and endure the terror of perceiving the enormity—in Leverkühn and in the century itself—of the spirit's simultaneous striving and vanishing. Mann finally is offering the reader the opportunity to play a central and unusual role (the modern role we have described) in the dynamics of the novel's vision, the opportunity—in Nietzschean terms—to be the novel's silent and essential hero.

The dissonant form of *Doctor Faustus* evokes and explores the freed, challenged consciousness of its reader condemned to experience the carnage and disillusionment which possess our century. The paradox of Mann's narrative is a powerful and conclusive figuring of the dissonant paradox I have been examining: the celebration of a desperately parodied, visionary humanism coincides with the revelation that it is a function of a travesty and vanishing of the human, of a self-disintegrating fiction. Or, in the words Mann gives Kretchmar, "music's deepest wish" is "not to be heard at all, not seen, not yet felt; but only—if that were possible—in some Beyond" (61). Linked in these terms and phrases to Adorno's thinking, Mann's novel gives form to a utopian yearning that is joined to a critical vision of its time and place in modernity. The modernist struggle in Mann's novel—as in Leverkühn's imagined music, in Adorno's thought, and we shall see in Joyce's comedy—is dangerously to locate the "human" on an earth reseen, reclaimed "in some Beyond"—that is, in the responsibility explicitly borne by the imagined future, by the reader. The reader's crucial engagement of the novel's dissonant form reveals the hidden and inevitable assumption underlying the use of a musical analogy in studies of *Doctor Faustus* and in the study of modern fiction generally. Mann is using a musical form that places its reader at its center, where he is relied on to perceive and sustain an affirmation the possibility of which the novelist's experimental irony envisions and subverts. It is an expression of paradoxical, pessimistic hope about the condition of art and man's spirit that this affirmation vitally and ultimately depends on the spirit—the depth of humanity and critical perception—of his reader.

7
Music and Modern British Fiction: Dissonant *Ulysses*— A Study of How to Read Joyce

I

As one surveys the terrain of dissonance in modern fiction, and particularly as I look now to the world that Joyce imagines, the lay and boundaries of this region of modernism become clear, its patterns and dynamic increasingly apparent. For example, Proust's reader experiences the challenge of a self-consciously musicalized narrative which is focused on the artist himself. Proust would ideally make each character or action in *À la recherche* into an exfoliating and enlarging spiritual possibility within the artist/narrator's encompassing imagination. The narrator's apparent goal is to create a solacing, Schopenhauerian sense of musicalized transcendence out of what is shown to be a life of disintegration; yet Proust's deeper achievement is to create a dissonant and unstable narrative challenging the reader to comprehend and explore the distortions and ambiguities in its unfoldings of identity and society.

Joyce, too, extends his narrative perspective beyond the persona of the artist—to the creation of Bloom and beyond in *Ulysses*, his greatest work. The vision of consciousness here is not formulated only by the illumination, however enlarged or profound, of Stephen Dedalus's rigid and defensive mask. Like Proust, Joyce insists on recreating his own life in art, his modern "alienated" experience, but in contrast to Proust, he imposes a fertile, parodying, vengefully extensive playfulness and particularity on his far more fractured, comically inventive creation—in *Ulysses*—of the urban reality of 16 June 1904, in Dublin and environs.

The practice I will trace in Joyce, of fomenting comic play and distortion in his imaginative world, is closely related to Mann's self-consciously dissonant art. The parodic dissonance in his fiction is a risk-taking attempt to construct an affirmation of enduring consciousness out of the disorder of his time. Mann's work seeks to enable the reader to affirm his own capacity to perceive and explore such disorder. The connection of musical dissonance to Joyce's fiction is forecast here by a comparison between Mann's and Joyce's ironic practices. Neither novelist seeks a "pure" music in prose, an ideal and transcendent unity of form which their fictions treat ironically. For Mann, irony is the dissonant voice of a fragmented yet enduring consciousness, a tragi-comic, often travestying form that infuses *Doctor Faustus*, for example, with involuted irony and parody. The formal dissonance of the latter novel arises from both a strategy of desperate parody assaulting, yet relying on the reader's engagement, and a related temporal strategy in which the events of the Second World War impinge on the fictive composition of the narrative even as it reaches toward the war.

In creating the dissonant counterpoint of *Doctor Faustus*—an imagined world in which the fragmenting impact of "reality" calls the forms of consciousness into question—Mann's aim is specifically to convey the weight of disintegration bearing on all the modern edifice of art and culture. In so doing, he reveals two interrelated means of creating art's "success," its difficult affirmation of the human out of the modern situation of the spirit, and those means are relevant to an understanding of Joyce's art. The first is the "negative" transcendence of parody, the desperate yet comic jump for Mann into the distorted heart of consciousness and experience. Given Mann's understanding of the necessity to take that comic risk, it is no accident that after the affirmation *through* travesty in Faustus he wrote the completion of *Felix Krüll*. The second means Mann employs is, as I argued earlier, to make the dissonant ambiguities—the desperate affirmation and comic risk—of his art reach out to involve, reveal and, ultimately, rely on the reader's own inner survival. These aesthetic means and, indeed, aims find their most extraordinary embodiment in Joyce's achievement.

That achievement is forecast and paralleled also by other modern novelists writing in English. For example, Conrad's formulation of fragmenting identity, of defensive and collapsing narrative strategies, of implacably opposed values—East and West—is designed to evoke from the reader a crucial exercise of perception and judgment central to the novelist's aim. Again for Conrad, fiction must not simply achieve a self-contained, aesthetic transcendence but, instead, aims to confront and activate the reader through its "sinister resonance" of ambiguous, subversive meaning assaulting him—a dissonance requiring the reader's own self-implicating judgment. Such discord—with its strategic impact on the reader—is apparent also in E. M. Forster's fiction. His speculations on music, as a model for the open-ended "expansion" of the conventional form and impact of fiction, illuminate his own novels (these comments are to be found in *Aspects of the Novel* as well as other of his essays, and in his notes on Beethoven's sonatas at Kings College, Cambridge).[1] Particularly *Howards End*, *A Passage to India*, and certain late stories in *The Life to Come*, achieve the "sinister resonance" which calls into question bourgeois complacency in the reader's response and subverts the novelist's own alternative allegiance to elegant harmonies of voice and structure (Alan Wilde—among others—offers insightful readings of that questioning and subversion, readings apart from, yet parallel to, the insights of a dissonant aesthetic).[2] In addition, Forster builds into his fiction references to musical models of simultaneously subversive and affirming form—Beethoven's Fifth, or Godbole's song, which achieve the confrontative impact of dissonance on Helen Schlegel and on Mrs. Moore and Fielding, each an imperfect yet searching surrogate and model for Forster's reader.

Virginia Woolf also laces her fiction with musical references—most concertedly in *The Waves* whose structure and premise are themselves musical, as Gerald Levin has demonstrated.[3] Yet Woolf's overt idealization of music as a Paterian, finally mythic solace and escape, clashes profoundly with the distress of consciousness her musicalized narratives covertly and actually reveal. Her fictional project is affected by a lack of awareness of its own promised power; the potential outpourings of consciousness—Bernard's and the others', or in the Joyce-influenced *Mrs Dalloway* Clarissa's and Septimus's[4]—are partly blocked by the restraints of her class-bound range and narrative sensibility and by the self-deception or at least confusion in her essential narrative strategy: Woolf would valorize a mannered aesthetic harmony which in actuality has vanished from her time and art.

As D. H. Lawrence confronts a similar cultural and aesthetic struggle, he attempts to wrest narrative structure—in character, plot, and language—from the grip of conventions like the locutions of class or other clichés of earlier novelistic practice. Rhythm in the novel, for him even more than for Forster, is a term meaning the fictive form and impact which confronts the conventional language of fiction with a call for the reader to exercise critical freedom in perception, in experience, in speech itself. Rhythm is the admission into fiction's language of "the pulsing, frictional to-and-fro" of "every natural crisis."[5] Indeed, rhythm is one musical term for fiction's acquisition of a new language in which symbolic image and incident intrude on the social surface of experience, to reorder and critically reveal its meaning. The process—exhibited best in *Women in Love's* brilliant fullness of image, like lanterns lit in utter darkness—is an explosive process, and the deepest musical analogy for it, I believe, is dissonance. The dissonance of Lawrence's fiction is its formulation of crisis, of the tension between freedom and dead convention, between, on the one hand, the essential carbon of what Lawrence calls "incarnate self," and on the other hand, the deceptive social display of ordinary self.[6] In moribund modernity, the potential for a wholeness of self and desire is an "unspeakable" potential, and yet Lawrence faces the obligation—as Leo Bersani among others suggests—to speak it, to juxtapose it to and root it in images from ordinary existence.[7]

The rifts and seams showing in Lawrence's best works—the awkward and distorting intensities—signal the difficulty of his task. They are signs of the intentional risk, the dissonance, of his struggle to imagine how full consciousness coexists with and subverts the deadening precepts and perspective assumed by modern society. Lawrence's urgent forms—their pressure on the reader to "reconstitute the self," in Langbaum's phrase[8]—share Joyce's aims, even as their anger or celebration differ from the force and brilliant play of what I would call Joycean dissonance. Each is in the vanguard of modernism, as Philip Weinstein suggests: "Lawrence and Joyce, faithful to the conditions of incarnate life, begin the job of dismantling the idols, one through attack and the other through play."[9]

The power of Joyce's fiction is in the complexity of its ambition—ranging beyond Lawrence's. The triple ambition of Joyce's greatest work, *Ulysses*, is that it paradoxically combines a faithfulness to the particularity and "incarnate" fullness of its imagined lives with an assault on the ordering conventions marking those lives, and above all with an encompassing playfulness which asserts the creative fictionality of both order and life. Joyce's play with paradox, moving also beyond Mann's play with time and travesty, is the essential, indeed Dionysian challenge of his dissonance—the locating of "reality" in "fiction," of spiritual survival in a spiritually paralyzed time, and of faithfulness to life within the grotesque.

For Joyce, Ireland is the particular region of such paradox and dissonance. He conceives of his fiction, as would an alien exiled in Europe and employing its vantage point as an instrument with which to measure the alienated existence—requiring some form beyond satire—of the island and city he had left. "Ireland was Joyce's fate," Thomas Flanagan writes, "a condition of his being with which he could come to terms only through rebellion."[10] And it is the essence of Joyce's dissonant form that, as the wily art of his exile, it transforms the act of rebellion into an affirmation. This is, indeed, the ultimate and deeply sought transformation for Irish modernists generally, and Yeats attempts it, for example in *Words to Music, Perhaps*. There we find Crazy Jane's great, sexualized, lyric rebuttal to the repressed bishop for whom the notion is anathema that the disordered process of living should be welcomed, let alone yield a unity of being. "'Love,'" she tells him, "'has pitched his mansion in / The place of excrement.'"[11]

Like Crazy Jane—only not in lyric isolation, but in an Ireland-encompassing and world-rivaling fiction—Joyce's *Ulysses* stirs in the reader this challenging insight: that the low and uncontrolled, the irrational heart and excremental part, are vital to the process of our noblest, most transcendent desire, of love, and alternatively that culture's variously hallowed images can shape, even as they are shaped by, the moments of our animality. The "dialogue" among these paradoxical yea-sayings is illuminated by the Nietzschean ideas of dissonance and the Dionysian. Joyce's discordant artifice enables the reader to encompass and freely explore the full world of self and culture, body and language, in their continual disintegration and resurgence. (Joyce's dialogue of yeses is also discussed in Jacques

Derrida's exploration of *Ulysses*.[12] Given the novel's sonorous and discordant dialogue of fictive affirmations, Derrida writes, "I hear this vibration as the very music" of the text.)[13] Music is more than the basis of allusion or of oblique influence for Joyce. It can provide us with an analogy and an aesthetic illuminating Joyce's aims and, most important, the impact of dissonant *Ulysses*.

II

As a young man, Joyce—with his active interest in fin de siècle aesthetics—read Arthur Symons's classic study of the Symbolists, *The Symbolist Movement in Literature*.[14] Like Mallarmé in Symons's portrait, the novelist aimed at completing the work of Wagner. This is not to say only that he would create a fiction-encompassing structure of leitmotifs, an extension of Dujardin's early stream of consciousness experiment, which the young Joyce also read. The structures and intentions of *Ulysses* above all embody and transform Wagnerian dissonance, a crucial and—for modern music—the most significant element of his music. As we have seen, Nietzsche construes Wagner's dissonance as the musical form which strives to mediate between disillusioning reality and the pure expressivity of art's Apollonian images; in these terms, Joyce's art becomes dissonant, for the crucial insight of the dissonant imagination is that the "sluggish matter" of the artist's life—and of modern life generally, disintegrating and in disorder—is a force in the aesthetic process: life's disillusioning collapse into the mutliple and fragmentary can be integrated as dissonance into art's form.

How does the experience of dissonance involve the reader, who is engaged in the process of understanding and judging the difficulties of *Ulysses*? The work's experimental narrative marks a radical withdrawal from conventional sense and form into cryptic idiosyncracy, difficult and oblique complexity, comic ambiguity and parody. That its forms may be grotesque or meaningless to the reader—may seem to be the death throes of fiction's language—is the danger of dissonance in fiction, yet the underlying aim of the dissonant qualities of *Ulysses* is that they should draw the reader into an innovative relationship to the novel. In the aesthetic I explore, the flux of dissonance assaults the perceiver with its obscurity, complexity, and ambiguity, with the difficult vitality of its formulation of existence.

As the reader penetrates the difficulties of the novel, the aim of the work is that he will find insight and delight now in the freed activity of his own engaged response. In Nietzschean terms, the dissonance of *Ulysses* involves the reader in the processes of perception and judgment by which human life may endure in a disordered world. Such are the claims of dissonance, and they constitute a key aspect of the forms we encounter in *Ulysses*.

Joyce's sense of the nature and power of an art modeled on music is, from the start, a significant element in his thought and work. Joyce himself sang, with a fine tenor voice, and as a novelist he found delight in weaving patterns of allusion to songs, operas, and other music through his work. The flow of plentiful allusion here is a subject already well and richly analyzed by Zack Bowen and, before him, by Hodgard and Worthington.[15] My interest is, instead, in the bearing of the aesthetics of music and particularly the idea of dissonance on Joyce's work. Of special relevance in this regard is the view of art that Stephen Dedalus is made to hold. Stephen presents us with Joyce's theory of art and of the capacity for literary creation though, indeed, not with the engaged perception and sensibility which underlie the act of creation itself (Bloom unwittingly embodies such a sensibility in *Ulysses*); nevertheless, in Stephen, Joyce presents the theoretical equipment for creation with its revelatory connection to a musical aesthetic.

From the earliest period of his artistic vocation, Joyce stood in close but radical relation to the main currents of late nineteenth-century European art, and he was profoundly influenced by its conception of music and especially Wagner's music (John DiGaetani offers a detailed, useful portrait of the European influence I discuss here).[16] As Joyce's preeminent biographer, Richard Ellmann, points out, the young writer's letter to Ibsen was a key assertion for Joyce of a European identity.[17] As an outsider from provincial Ireland who revolted against its imperfections and reached out to the spiritual life of Europe, he grasped and made use of the two elemental forces of the period: the dramatic spirit of Ibsen and Wagner, and the lyric spirit of the French Symbolists. These two forces are united in their basic significance for Joyce, in being the tools of his rebellion but also in the concern they display with a musical paradigm for art.

Joyce's earliest work, *Chamber Music*, suggests the symbolist influence in particular. "The chief axiom" that Joyce took from the

Symons study of symbolism "was that expressed most memorably by Walter Pater: 'All art aspires constantly to the condition of music.'"[18] Joyce's early poems are marked above all by a concern with musical metaphors and a musical subject. They do not attempt, as do the later works, "dramatically" and ironically to engage the ideal of musical form he here embraces (though the pun in the title points toward the future). As a result, these poems are a weak attempt to evoke a world of personal symbols and intensities, "an inner world of individual emotions mirrored perfectly" by a lyricism that Joyce found in Verlaine (the phrase is Stephen's in *A Portrait*).[19] Though he does not admit the tension between reality and the lyric ideal into these poems, the important value of that ideal remains a force, however transformed, in his later fiction. (Relevant here is Blanchot's and Adorno's call—noted in chapter 2—for the lyric "I" to give way to the opportunities of narrative.) Joyce's early essay on Mangan describes the lyric ideal and, there, uses terms from the symbolist conception of music (the passage is repeated in *Stephen Hero*):

> A song by Shakespeare or Verlaine, which seems so free and living and as remote from any conscious purpose as rain that falls in a garden or the lights of evening, is discovered to be the rhythmic speech of an emotion otherwise incommunicable, at least not so fitly.[20]

The attempt to capture the rhythmic speech of an emotion is the aim which the symbolists, Pater, and Ezra Pound have described, and that aim finally underlies the view of Joyce's last experiment which Beckett asserts: *Finnegans Wake* "is not about something; it is that something itself"—a pure expressivity formed by means of a musically conceived art.[21]

Joyce's early interest in a musical conception of literary art is best revealed in *A Portrait of the Artist as a Young Man*. There, Stephen's interest in music points to Joyce's own sensitivity to musical form. Stephen is obsessed by the power of song and the voice itself (for example, his father's voice in their sojourn together in Cork). The song becomes a revelation of the inner nature of the singer. Because musical form has that power of revelation, this youthful Irish symbolist conceives of music as an image of ideal art (in such art, "words harmonize in a chord"). Joyce portrays the autobiographical artist as a fine tenor, yet the angle of the portrait reveals that Stephen's deepest interest in music is literary and is marked by the self-indulgent posturing of the spiritually tortured would-be artist.

For Stephen, the relationship of art to reality ideally depends on the moments of revelation (of epiphany in Joyce's early terminology) which transform and transcend "the sluggish matter" of existence; with a certain arrogance, he sees art as a sacramental recapturing of such moments, as a transcendence through them of a painful and intolerable reality. Yet Stephen is also tortured emotionally as he moves back and forth between an unfulfilled commitment to such art and the impure reality which he rejects with pride and irony as he experiences it.

In chapter 4 of *A Portrait*, the climactic scene, in which Stephen struggles to an awareness of his proud calling, is built around both musical images and a sense of the musical quality of the European art to which he wants to reach out and commit himself. At one point, the art Stephen feels called to create specifically calls to him from the Continent:

> The Europe they had come from lay out there beyond the Irish Sea. . . . He heard a confused music within him as of memories and names which he was almost conscious of but could not capture even for an instant; then the music seemed to recede, to recede, to recede: and from each receding trail of nebulous music there fell away one long drawn calling note.[22]

The call is in reality that of his companions shouting his name, Dedalus. Was that cry, Stephen imagines, not "a symbol of the artist forging anew in his workshop out of the sluggish matter of the earth a new soaring impalpable imperishable being?"

The ironies here are centered on exactly the sluggish matter surrounding Stephen and existing within the adolescent, egotistical and insecure musings he would make "harmonious" and sublime. What may be harmonious for Stephen is not always so for Joyce or his reader, and indeed the music to be heard from Europe at century's end provoked rather than confirmed. Such ironies govern the transitions throughout *A Portrait*, from word to word, paragraph to paragraph, and chapter to chapter. A coexisting irony and spiritual self-affirmation in Stephen's experience are at the core of Joyce's vision and of the reader's engaged apprehension; in this way, the narrative reveals the profoundly disjunctive nature of a struggling soul's experience of reality. Organically expressive "rhythmic speech" in literature is only a part of the art Joyce practices here rendering the complex inward voice of Stephen's striving spirit. And it is only a part of the European spirit towards which Stephen reaches, only a first step toward what is finally Joyce's narrative dissonance—the goal of dramatically objectifying the artist's experience of world and self.

III

"Stephen's description of 'dramatic art,'" S. L. Goldberg writes in *The Classical Temper*, "is a more sensible variation of the symbolist formula that all art aspires to the condition of music," a formula which Joyce has "translated into terms that include the drama and the novel as well as the lyric."[23] This perception indicates that the idea of an organically expressive musical art is not abandoned but transformed by Joyce's use of a dramatic paradigm, and the rhythmic speech of art's language for the self becomes no longer a vehicle for personal self-expression but a means for objectifying the artist's inner experience; thus, Joyce makes the "impure" fictionalized reality of that experience subject to musical formulation. Joyce's development of the symbolist ideal here moves toward the conception of dissonance.

Stephen asserts the dramatic conception of art in *A Portrait* when, in the chapter following the scene discussed above, he talks with Lynch:

> The esthetic image in the dramatic form is life purified in and reprojected from the human imagination. The mystery of esthetic like that of material creation is accomplished. The artist, like the God of his creation, remains within or behind or beyond or above his handiwork, invisible, refined out of existence, indifferent, paring his fingernails.
> —Trying to refine them also out of existence, said Lynch.[24]

The intentionally discordant dualities of the passage range from Lynch's ironic antiphony through the fact that Stephen's view of dramatic form is, in part, a defensive maneuver, an assertion of the aesthetic and spiritual ideal opposed to the reality which entrenches it; and those ironic dualities culminate in Joyce's serio-comic embodiment here of the dramatic form that Stephen is trying to assert.

The connection between Joyce's use of dramatic form and the nature of dissonance becomes clear when we recognize and examine how Stephen's idea of drama finds its origin and parallel in the European art that calls to him. Joyce himself offers us that recognition and points to the connection between drama and dissonance in his essay "Drama and Life" written when he was eighteen; the essay, in large part on Ibsen, asserts that Wagner and Ibsen share the same aesthetic aim and a similar ideal of form.

> The creator in Ibsen forgoes his very self and stands a mediator in awful truth before the veiled face of God [that also impersonal creator].... Drama is again the least dependent of all arts on its material [and its source within the artist's mind. For] drama arises spontaneously out of life and is coeval with it. Every race has made its own myths and it is in these that early drama often finds an outlet. The author of Parsifal has recognized this and hence his work is solid as a rock.[25]

Joyce points not to the leitmotif in Wagner as the source of his importance. Instead, many times in this and other early essays, he connects Wagner with Ibsen in terms of their molding of a new dramatic form which gives "universal import" to action played out in seclusion or in the "common parlour" itself—an art form that makes of such action a "world drama."[26] The admission of the "common" and ironic, of the realities of collapse and of feeling itself, into the world of aesthetic, "mythic" ideals is achieved, above all, by dissonance; in Nietzschean terms, dissonant form is a most powerful modern exemplum of dramatic form, as each mediates between a spiritual ideal and disillusioning experience, above all by embodying the tension between them. Such form voices the alienated tension between expectation and reality which informs modern consciousness and, in Nietzsche's argument, the life of classical Greek culture onwards. In this sense, dramatic and dissonant form are the same as—to use Joyce's phrase once again—they arise "spontaneously out of life" to find a place in the "coeval" world of art. As I argue in chapter 4, Nietzsche's analysis of Wagner's relation to Greek tragic drama provides a source and rationale for the view of dramatic form that Joyce developed. The works of Wagner and Ibsen offered examples of the dissonant form and spirit with which the musicalized novels of Joyce (like those of Proust and Mann) self-consciously experiment.

In *A Portrait* and even more so in *Ulysses*, Joyce not only transforms the thrust of idealized "myth" into a dramatically complex rendering, a dissonant rendering of reality itself (i.e., into an ironic, still vital "fiction"). Also, he radically expands the use of the symbolist ideal of musical form in order to render through dissonance the reality it would transcend; the Dedalean artist, bearing the chalice of the symbolist image, stumbles to earth, into time, and indeed toward a dissonant aesthetic. Narrative dissonance is the temporal form which would unite the spiritual desire for transcendence with the sluggish matter of "reality" where the spiritual aspirations of the self arise, where desire "has pitched his mansion." Joyce's dissonant union of irony and exactly rendered feeling and consciousness, his paradoxical fusion of reality and spirit, of outer and inner experience, creates a fiction which, like life, assaults the perceiver with its complex vitality, with the demystifying yet affirmative power of its formulation of existence.

A cornerstone of the Nietzschean view of dissonance is that such a formulation reveals the disintegration besetting modern consciousness *in order to* stir to life in the perceiver an investment of creative energy, of fiction-engaging and self-forming capacity. In this regard, Joyce writes in an early essay of the perceiver's experience of dramatic form which is a dissonant transformation of the musical ideal he first avowed: "When the art of a dramatist is perfect the critic is superfluous. Life is not to be criticized, but to be faced and lived."[27]

Joyce's claim for art's effect on the reader/perceiver, that it moves beyond transcendent abstraction toward confrontation, is closely tied to the musical aesthetic Nietzsche develops; it is the claim of dissonance.

Joyce taps a source of modernism when, in his own terms, he engages and transforms the views of musical form that the Symbolists, Wagner, and Nietzsche differently develop. Here let me specify how his use of those insights underlies and illuminates the form and impact of *A Portrait* itself. The musically conceived rhythms of Stephen's consciousness are precisely realized as the rhythmic speech, the unfolding forms of Joyce's prose, and those forms are simultaneously a dissonant embodiment of his consciousness; they objectify the vital yet provisional and conflicting fictions unfolding within the envisioned self. As I noted in the scene of Stephen's vocation and that with Lynch, the discordant "truths" of Stephen's experience—his aspirations in conflict with his actual situation—make up the dissonance of Joyce's rendering of consciousness. The dissonant form of the novel also asserts a new view of character in fiction, for as Joyce stands above the artwork constructing and mediating between the simultaneous and conflicting elements of Stephen's existence, he is objectifying the multiple truths of his own self and his own perception of the human spirit. And Joyce's art in this way renders the vital rhythms and tensions within the self and asserts his capacity to explore the unfolding fictions of the self and to choose among them.

The dissonance of *A Portrait* also requires of the reader a radical engagement of its vision which is—in Joyce's early rhetoric—"to be faced and lived"; that is, the reader is obliged to explore and judge the world of human possibility—and multiplicity—that Joyce there envisions. In this perspective, the critical opposition between sympathetic and ironic readings of *A Portrait* moves toward a resolution, for example, of two polar critical responses or readings. Hugh Kenner, in one view (formulated early in his career), suggests that even as Joyce seems to move beyond the rebellious heroics voiced in Stephen's avowal of an "Ibsen-Wagner-Nietzsche image of . . . life," the novelist takes up the spiritual strategies and aesthetic procedures that issue from that axis of influences.[28] This reading proposes that Joyce takes up those forms and aims in order to create a negative, ironic vision of his autobiographical "hero's" spiritual failures. Kenner is stunned out of sympathy with Stephen's struggle by the spectre Joyce evokes of the degradation of modern life and the dying of former order. Yet the Nietzschean "image of life" and of dissonant art points to another reading of Joyce's irony. For in exercising the "rebellious" freedom to forge a self out of his modern experience, Joyce himself confronts the resulting distortions in the modern spirit and affirms them as part of the dissonant life of his vision.

In this alternative view of Joyce's self- and world-encompassing irony, his dissonant form achieves the continued life of the self by embodying the tension between disillusioning reality and spiritual transcendence in the narrative of Stephen's growth. The novel's form, with its balance of irony and sympathy, requires that the reader comprehend, a simultaneity of opposed perceptions and judgments of Stephen (later I examine a poststructuralist version of this conception with regard to *Ulysses*). The dissonance of the novel is Joyce's means to draw from us a creative participation in that process of imaginative perception, of constructing the fiction's meaning. The novelist here challenges us to form a self-implicating meaning from the simultaneity of conflicting responses evoked from us, and we thus are made to "face" his vision as a lifelike embodiment of the complexity informing our own inner and outer reality. His dissonant form obliges us actively to engage a fiction out of which we create our own human identity. The reader's participation in that process of imaginative confrontation and creation reveals to him the mechanisms and the risks implicit in how the self is formed, how consciousness endures. In this way, Joyce not only affirms the continued, if embattled, life of the self in our century; he also affirms, in Richard Ellmann's phrase, the love of that life as he makes the reader participate in the creative process by which he "mothers and fathers" the growth of his own multifarious identity.[29]

IV

An understanding of dissonant form in *Ulysses* helps to resolve the central question the novel's reader faces, of the meaning—empty or enlivening—of Joyce's immense experimental artifice and of the author's aesthetic distance from his creation, from its "human context." How does the reader judge the sometimes apparent triviality of parody in *Ulysses*, the impingement there of Dublin reality on Joyce's vision, or the clash of parallel levels of unfolding meanings—the clash of Homeric and urban contexts, the simultaneous voicing of sarcasm and sympathy, of irony and affirmation? To analyze how the idea of a dissonant *Ulysses* helps to resolve such questions, let me first take up one of the more problematic episodes in the novel, "Sirens," which raises also the question of a musical model for fiction. In this regard, we confront linked questions about both the degree to which, in Karen Lawrence's phrase, "language is and is not music" and the degree to which "the drama of writing usurps the dramatic action."[30]

What is the dissonance of the Music Room scene with its literary counterpoint of fragmentary, strategically "jingling" phrases? The phrases stated on the first pages establish thematic and linguistic associations within the episode, and those phrases are repeatedly integrated, with often absurd effects, into the episode's narrative structure. The narrative itself contains and reveals the multiple levels of Bloom's associations, the unfolding action, and parodied myth. Readers have faulted the counterpoint which results from this integration of structures: it has seemed labored in technique and lacking in narrative power. Yet the episode is not ponderous; it is an often humorous counterpoint of ambiguities—a discordant, indeed comic "music." At work here are the ingenious effects of Joyce's tricky, often comic literary play, his sense of the possibilities of language. Joyce here introduces dissonance into the classical principles of stylistic decorum, as Hugh Kenner demonstrates in *Joyce's Voices*.[31] Subsequent criticism has fully explored the episode's travestying of rhetoric among other Joycean obsessions (see, for example, the "Sirens Without Music" essays in the centennial collection edited by Morris Beja).[32] Yet Bloom's sensibility remains at the center of the episode; that is, his perception of the bar at four in the afternoon, of the men and women there, of the songs sung, and of Blazes Boylan's four o'clock meeting with Molly. The scene's dissonant counterpoint continues to develop the multiple, often grotesque, human truths of Bloom's situation—body, mind, heart, spirit, and all. The narrative artifice simultaneously victimizes and enhances the stream of Bloom's consciousness. At one climax to the episode, Bloom perceives the high tenor note Simon sings in the aria "M'appari."

> —Co-me, thou lost one!
> Co-me thou dear one!
> Alone. One love. One hope. One comfort me. Martha, chest-note, return.
> Come!
> It soared, a bird, it held its flight, a swift pure cry, soar silver orb it leaped serene, speeding, sustained, to come, don't spin it out too long long breath he breath long life, soaring high, high resplendent, aflame, crowned, high in the effulgence symbolistic, high, of the ethereal bosom, high, of the high vast irradiation everywhere all soaring all around about the all, the endlessnessnessness.
> To me!
> Siopold![33]

Joyce's irony is in putting the parody of "effulgent," baroque, self-consciously "musical" prose into Bloom's mental process as he thinks: "don't spin it out too long." "Too long long," this passage also strives simultaneously to communicate the intensity of Bloom's experience, the involvement which issues in his creative identification with the operatic character Lionel and the singer Simon: "Siopold!" The portmanteau word contains both the comic deflation of the already parodied "high" prose as well as the complexity of Bloom's experience. It can be argued that music is not the deepest model for Joyce's effects since the music here seems cut off from Bloom's "apprehension of self"; as Bloom listens in this sequence—Cheryl Herr suggests—"the self stirs to play only a highly conventional score."[34] As well, Bloom's intuitive and fluctuating responsiveness to music—"Siopold!"—"threatens to dissolve Bloom to the state of semiotic mush."[35] Yet, this last is precisely the point: Bloom's role here is indeed to be a highly receptive, indeed gifted listener to scores, conventional and otherwise; his human and imaginative openness is confirmed even in the midst of clichéd conventions. Moreover, Joyce's own listener/reader in "Sirens" must face the further challenge of an unconventional text which can stir the self to play—to explore—an unconventional score.

The dissonant structures of the section place the reader in the crucial position of perceiving the radical distortions of its musical form but also the vitality of life that endures there—which its dissonance voices. The meaning and value of that dissonant counterpoint, therefore, depends on the reader himself, sorting out the ambiguities and penetrating to the still human voice within that dissonance. Our engagement of the novel—an involvement of perception and human judgment on which the work's value depends—is, potentially, a version of Bloom's involvement with music above, only conscious of the distortion and, indeed, the imaginative risk of self involved in our response: "Siopold!" Joyce's art here is, finally, a far more experimental example of the strategy of dissonance, of ironic transcendence and desperate parody, by which Thomas Mann's work also challenges the reader to take up his crucial role.

In *Ulysses*, the full-fledged voicing of discordant structures both possesses and subverts the imagined flux of consciousness. Joyce's dissonance finally reveals how the modern striving of the spirit—modern consciousness with its overweening aspirations and its failed unities and ideals—endures only as it is engaged and measured by our humanity. Like what Mann calls the "serious jest" of his dissonant art, then, the dissonant form of *Ulysses* takes up the unfolding elements of the self and shows how they survive in a world of disintegrating spirit. A crucial aspect of the larger dissonance of the novel is the exuberant, comic voice of disintegration in Joyce's rendering of modern consciousness—for example: the madly inclusive lists as in "Cyclops," the arbitrary inclusion of the author's name as a bike rider's, the expressionist battering of the characters' inner worlds in "Circe," along with many violations elsewhere of their sense of self, the clash of narrative consciousness throughout (for instance, in the neatly halved "Nausica"), the "endless" parodies, and the private grudges and trivial "borrowings" from Dublin reality which intentionally disrupt (as R. M. Adams's *Surface and Symbol* points out[36]) scholars' compulsive attempts to see a paradigmatic and transcendent order in the aesthetic surface of *Ulysses*. As Frank Kermode suggests in *The Sense of an Ending*:

> *Ulysses* studies and develops the tension between paradigm and reality, asserts the resistance of fact to fiction, human freedom and unpredictability against plot. Joyce chooses a Day; it is a crisis ironically treated. The day is full of randomness. There are coincidences, meetings that have point, and coincidences which do not. We might ask whether one of the merits of the book is not its lack of mythologizing.[37]

The comedy of Joyce's dissonance is not the stoic comedy of an ideal, mythic spirit imprisoned in a world of human debris; his work "transcends" such a negation because the novel envisions the survival of the human spirit not as opposed to but within the distorted, parodied, imperfect, temporal forms of modern consciousness. Joyce's comedy formulates a disintegrating world in order to affirm the investment of imaginative energy that the assaulting form itself stirs to life in the reader. The energy he invests of a freed, critical engagement emerges from the parallel, dissonant engagement to be found in Nietzsche's emblem of the Dionysian, a singing, "music-practicing Socrates."[38] The aim of Joyce's dissonant comedy is to involve the reader in the process of imaginative perception and judgment by which human life endures in a world of disorder. The reader's "discovery of dissonance" (in Kermode's phrase) is his discovery of the freed, human response *Ulysses* renders and evokes from him.[39]

To return to the dissonance of the "Sirens" episode, Richard Ellmann, whose criticism profoundly enters into the affirmative spirit of the novel, points out in *Ulysses on the Liffey* that Bloom moves beyond the seductions of Dublin music, beyond the attraction of a vocal art divorced from reality, of a seemingly impotent language.[40] Yet, the music of the episode itself is not only that music of a Dublin "music room" and bar; the music of the text itself is a dissonant counterpoint which formulates the life-giving ironies of Joyce's vision. Bloom's musing that music—as "mathematical" as it seems—is the "language of love" sounds through that dissonance and is a part of it; as undercut as it is by its many contexts (for example, the fact that Simon is not the only tenor on Bloom's mind), his insight ironically but appropriately suggests Ellmann's penetrating understanding of the life and love affirming nature of Joyce's own art. As Ellmann states in his own terms, a profound feature of Joyce's dissonant comedy here is the way in which the author makes Bloom's consciousness accommodate, endure, and indeed affirm its still vital humanity within the imaginative world of parody, vacancy and the overweening spirit in which we, too, are made to discover our inner lives.

V

The dissonance of *Ulysses* formulates and embodies the connections among the characters' selves, Joyce's consciousness, and ourselves as readers. We saw that, in "Sirens," the inner life which in Bloom survives the episode's imaginative distortions is rendered by a dissonant language far more liberated, prodigal, and craftily disordered than the art of which, for example, Stephen conceives even as he points to the theoretical basis of Joyce's experiment. The imaginative life *Ulysses* bodies forth both in Bloom and enclosing his consciousness is disintegrating, violated by reality, yet enduring and still open to experience. Both the vitality and vacancy of Joyce's vision find their apotheosis in Molly's soliloquy, but they are embodied with the most sustained and complex power by Bloom who, unlike Stephen the spiritual tightrope artist, has the subjective experience of an intellectually baffled, incapable but sensual, and humane "everyman." Bloom is not only embattled by his experience as husband, father, and Irish Jew, but also symbolically flattened by the literary steamroller of the novel, the form of which paradoxically brings him into existence.

Joyce here illuminates his own embattled and complex spirit by creating Bloom as well as Stephen, characters who reveal the contradictory qualities of his inner experience as man and artist. The novel, R. M. Adams notes, "is, in part at least, a gambler's act of throwing his whole personality—his accidents, his skills, his weaknesses, his luck—against the world."[41] Joyce risks consciously creating his art from his discordances of self. He makes the two major male characters share habits and inner qualities that he had in youth and, then, in early middle age; finally, the day on which Stephen and Bloom find their existence in *Ulysses* and their connection there to Joyce is 16 June 1904, the day on which Joyce had a first meeting alone on Howth Hill with Nora Barnacle, the day marking the growth in him of a new sense of experience and the self.[42] In *Ulysses*, Joyce then places those characters embodying his vision of possibilities within the self into a literary context which itself embodies the freed but costly power of art to imagine the disintegrating nature of reality and the spirit in modern times.

Joyce's spiritual and autobiographical connection to unwitting Bloom finds its meaning and rationale illuminated by the conception of Joyce's dissonance. Dissonant form is a dramatic fostering of the essential quality of all musical form: its complex and suggestive "ambivalence" of content.[43] Joyce's dissonant art renders the complex and ambiguous rhythms and patterns constituting the self, revealing the world of conflicting spiritual possibilities which are the self. The envisioned multiplicity of self that we encounter in *Ulysses* includes Stephen who develops the theoretical capacity to create dissonant form, Bloom who has the sensibility to engage the spiritual work which dissonance formulates, and Molly whose voice is the vital flow of dissonance itself.

In "Circe," Stephen is made to voice the connection I describe between musical form and Joyce's sense of the nature of the self. Stephen equates the movement of musical intervals through the scale with the multiplicity of selves which unfold in individual experience and, particularly, within the artist's. Here, in musical terms, Stephen restates the theory of art he developed in "Scylla and Charybdis": Shakespeare becomes the composite creator (both Bloomlike and Stephenlike), the consummate artist as cuckolded, godlike father of himself. Stephen's theory voices the intellectualizing youth's search for a form of negative capability—of Dionysian consciousness—by which he can, like that god and like Shakespeare, imaginatively enter the world of experience. His search is for at least the theoretical means to achieve the growth of a spirit like Bloom's within him, to allow the unfolding of multiple possibilities in existence—Hellenic, Hebraic, and beyond:

THE CAP OF LYNCH

... Jewgreek is greekjew. Extremes meet. Death is the highest form of life. Bah!

STEPHEN

You remember fairly accurately all my errors, boasts, mistakes. ... Here's another for you. (*He frowns.*) The reason is because the fundamental and the dominant are separated by the greatest possible interval which ...

THE CAP

Which? Finish. You can't.

STEPHEN

(*With an effort.*) Interval which. Is the greatest possible ellipse. Consistent with. The ultimate return. The octave. Which.

THE CAP

Which?

(*Outside the gramophone begins to blare* The Holy City.)

STEPHEN

(*Abruptly.*) What went forth to the ends of the world to traverse not itself. God, the sun, Shakespeare, a commercial traveller, having itself traversed in reality itself, becomes that self. Wait a moment. Wait a second. Damn that fellow's noise in the street. Self which it itself was ineluctably preconditioned to become. Ecco! (411–12)

"That fellow's" recurring shout in the novel is an arbitrary vestige of the human spirit, a time bound, attenuated god. Since time with its disasters and opportunities will not "wait a second," only the temporal form of a dissonant art can accommodate and formulate the risks and distortions of human consciousness in such a time, with such a god.

In spite of the ironies that assault Stephen's fragmented consciousness here, however, his search for a multiplicity of selves—and human meanings—resounds through the text like the tonic and dominant of self and other, Bloom and Stephen both. Finally, Stephen's conception of multiple possibilities sounding together in art, exactly like the tones of an ultimately dissonant chord, is a key to the nature of Joyce's art. The opening up of the "scale" to all its tones enacts the emancipation of dissonance, and this notion is at the core of the analogy between dissonance and Joyce's freed play with fictive form and consciousness.

The novelist's aim is "to use words (and, finally, whole works) like musical chords saying several things at once at one instant"; these are the words of David Daiches who points to the neutralizing simultaneity—the comically deflating process of identification—in Joyce's musical effects which "break down any scale of values with which we may approach the work."[44] Exactly such effects, however, reveal how the human spirit can endure in a world where all is in doubt, and they strategically compel the reader to choose the fictions in which he invests significance. And, above all, those musical effects embody Joyce's richly innovative and vital conception of the self and of character in fiction. As Stephen's remarks in "Circe" suggest, musical form provides a rationale and a strategic model for Joyce's attempt to render the opposed elements of his own identity, the complexity of his own enduring inner life. The dissonant structure of the novel, then, enables Joyce to create his inner triangulation, and the novel's dissonant counterpoint ambiguously and obliquely connects Stephen and Bloom in identity and experience because the two characters are, finally, spiritual possibilities within Joyce himself, their "parallactic" destiny.

The most radical experiments in *Ulysses* and its most assaulting dissonance are found in "Circe" and the other later chapters. A comic simultaneity of sympathy and irony, of emotional expressivity and intellectual ingenuity or ridicule, is felt in the large gestures of these chapters and in their smallest details. What Stephen calls the tonic and dominant of Joyce's selves are surrounded by the unfolding dissonance of stylistic history in the hospital scene of "Oxen of the Sun," then of Circean metamorphoses of the unconscious life, and later—in "Ithaca"—by the dissonance of its reductive scientific catechism. The counterpointed, finally joined fates of Stephen and Bloom coexist, then, within the externally imposed, increasingly baroque, parodying narrative structures there.

Let me illustrate the way in which Joyce's effort to associate qualities of the two characters in "Circe" grows radically; the characters unconsciously receive a substantial share of each other's nature here, a symbolic and comic advance on their aesthetic destiny as multiple aspects of Joyce's vision of the self. Among such shared qualities contributing to the dissonant structure of the episode and the novel are the tag of jewgreek is greekjew, AE's bicycle pump, the gift to Stephen of watermelon (associated, as it is, with Bloom's experience of Molly), and the image of Stephen plus Bloom become horned Shakespeare in a mirror. In the last example, which is a climactic unfolding of one leitmotif in the novel, Shakespeare bids Bloom gaze into the enlivening and distorting mirror that Joyce has placed before him and Stephen; the dramatist's horned and paralyzed face says from within the mirror: "Thou thoughtest as how thou wastest invisible. Gaze" (463). With its grotesque distortions, the image in the mirror is created from and itself reflects Joyce's own multiple self, his sense of how the self survives in all its ironic complexity. With the demand that we exercise our freedom, our engaged perception and judgment, before its multiple and distorting vision, the mirror of Joyce's art is also made to engulf the reader. This image represents what is, in terms of the temporal structure of fiction, the dissonant power of *Ulysses*.

The connection between Stephen and Bloom—as an element of plot—is a random yet still resonant, distinctly modern meeting of human beings surviving with what resources of vitality and humanity they have amid the haunted and towering ruins of urban civilization. In the novel, Joyce's all-encompassing spirit itself dominates and possesses those ruined labyrinthine structures of modern consciousness, each mode of which the work ironically appropriates; and his multiple spirit—in the remarkable sense observable here—is the focus of underlying meaning for the meeting of the two characters. In "Eumaeus," as the two men navigate Dublin's streets at one o'clock in the morning, Bloom is made obliquely and unwittingly to describe the nature of the modern world Joyce envisions and in which they find their existence; he "jocosely" remarks to Stephen: "Our lives are in peril tonight. Beware the steamroller!" "Ithaca" is that peril, the steamroller flattening out living human beings into maps of themselves. Yet, our perception of the episode, and of Joyce's art in general, is not that it destroys human lives. Rather, his art reveals in what condition man's potentially vital and humane spirit survives in modern experience, what is at stake before the destructive forces in our spiritual world, and what affirmation is possible in such a world.

Joyce's affirmation of life is, finally, achieved by a dissonant art that simultaneously voices the comically multiple and opposed truths of his and our own inner experience.

Joyce's art here moves beyond the equally self-conscious "musical" efforts of Mann and Proust, both in the Irish novelist's more radical experiment with a dissonant language for consciousness and culture and, also, in his acceptance of the need to reveal the distorted yet vital multiplicity of self at the center of vision. He does not simply create an extended revelation of the "artist's" experience— attempting to celebrate his visionary triumph as does Proust or desperately and ironically controlling it as does Mann. Joyce's vision grows beyond the world of Faustus, of Marcel, and of Stephen himself, who is tortured in his struggle to affirm and explore experience through denial. Joyce's greater vision in *Ulysses* is his self-revealing engagement of the associative fantasies within Bloom and, finally, of the fickle yet unstoppable flow of human responsiveness in Molly Bloom. The novel affirms the sense of multiplicity, of the ceaseless fiction making and engaging energies within the immense variety of consciousness and self. *Ulysses* affirms the possibility for a vital, human engagement in the face of the reductive, irrational thrust that possesses modern consciousness. With the creation of Bloom and Molly, Joyce's vision of experience reveals how the self lives on in his time and how it may be affirmed even as it is profoundly assaulted by modern life.

VI

The unity of mythic and coherent intent that readers seek to identify in *Ulysses* is also what the reader recognizes as a self-conscious, multiple, and contingent *fiction*, a life-encompassing metaphor which bespeaks our hope and need for a unity achieved with difficulty. Finally, such unity and coherence are disclosed by *Ulysses* only as the reader, through an exercise of human insight and judgment, discovers in simultaneity of conflicting meanings in the novel the dissonant voice of his own enduring sense of self.

The dissonance of *Ulysses* is the challenging form which reaches out to include the reader's responses and place them at its center. Like drama as described in Joyce's early prose, a dissonant fiction is "to be faced and lived." The dissonance of his work, a radical development of the dissonant form and energies Nietzsche helps us to analyze, relies on the reader to master the complex and exfoliating ambiguities of its formulation of experience. As Fritz Senn, among other poststructuralist critics, has made clear, we, as readers, "have been composing the novel just as the author has done."[45] Its ambiguities in language and structure make *Ulysses* seem "to want to redress, emend, adjust, itself continually," and such textual instabilities inevitably involve "the reader in these processes."[46] As we thus learn to confront "decisions which no authority can make for us," we discern a new genealogy of morals in Joyce, revealing the potential for freed "becoming," for ontological freedom, in Joyce's post-Nietzschean transformation of fiction's form.[47] Finally, the value of the novel crucially depends on the reader's creative engagement of its ambiguities which both assault and formulate his sense of self; their value depends on one's creation from them, of a meaning that voices and affirms the survival of one's humanity within the modern world Joyce envisions. Leslie Fiedler's disarming acknowledgment is pertinent: that he has "been living Joyce for a long time now, and especially I have been living *Ulysses*, not outside of but within the very texture of my life, as a part of the process of growing up and growing old."[48]

With respect to the reader's role as in much else, Joyce's art is closely related to the development not only of a musical aesthetic for literature; it is illuminated also by the full dissonance of modern music itself. Claude Lévi-Strauss usefully describes the significance of the latter parallel, in a manner the limitations of which are revealing for his structuralist perspective, even as he forecasts certain features of the poststructuralism to follow. In *The Raw and the Cooked*, he writes that the modern "school" of atonal composers

> has chosen to risk its fate, and the fate of music, on a gamble. Either it will succeed in bridging the traditional gap between listener and composer and—by depriving the former of the possibility of referring unconsciously to a general system—will at the same time oblige him, if he is to understand the music he hears, to reproduce the individual act of creation on his own account. Through the power of an ever new, internal logic, each work will rouse the listener from his state of passivity to make him share in its impulse, so that there will no longer be a difference of kind, but only of degree, between inventing music and listening to it.[49]

Opposed to that experimental use of musical form—according to Lévi-Strauss—the structuralist use of musical form to order his study of "timeless" and transcendent myth. For the study of *Ulysses*, however, the central point remains that, in modern fiction as in modernist music, it is precisely dissonance that is the *temporal* form which ambiguously contains both the voice of our response to the present failure of the past languages of art, as well as the expressive forms out of which the perceiver is challenged to create an imagined organization of his own inner time and—finally—an affirmation of his enduring sense of self. *Ulysses*, with its vital connection to this Nietzschean conception of music, challenges the reader to take up that creative role at the center of its dissonant form.

Such dissonance and its effect constitute one basis for the connection in form and meaning between *Ulysses* and Joyce's final, most radical experiment. *Finnegans Wake* would become clear, Joyce thought, if the reader listened to its music; the novelist there challenges the reader to penetrate to the human expressivity of its protean, seemingly impenetrable surfaces, to the enduring vitality which its alien music formulates as it grows out of and transforms a time of disintegration. When the novelist directs the reader to open himself to the comic, cryptic and wondrous play of sound, rhythm, and syntax in the novel, he suggests his reliance on the reader to create his own sense of how the self endures from the multiple and disintegrating forms, the dissonant voicing of endless human possibility, at the *Wake*. As Northrop Frye suggests, the ultimate hero of Joyce's last novel is the reader.[50]

The ideal reader, as Joyce would have it, should devote an insomniac's lifetime to reading *Finnegans Wake*. This is not only an ironic reference to the unending literary and personal tricks that the author plays there and in *Ulysses*, particularly on scholars. Joyce is also suggesting that his last novel assaults the reader like life itself, fragmenting perception and challenging him to devote his existence to the creation of its meaning; the *Wake* indeed carries the challenge of dissonance to the point of extremity, of a characteristically modern extremity. Though the earlier novel does not have the ferocity of his final attack on and attempt to occupy the reader's consciousness, Joyce's full yet strategically tempered dissonance in *Ulysses* succeeds in drawing from the reader a crucial involvement of self—of insight and human judgment—and a corresponding act of imaginative creation. *Ulysses* is, finally, a life-giving fiction, for in our strategic engagement of its dissonant form, we are made to discover ourselves, our still vital sense of time and consciousness.

8
Conclusion: On the Discoveries of Dissonance in Modern Fiction

Dissonance offers a model of freedom and of the fictive for the understanding of modern narrative. The audacious wit and passion deployed in modern texts are projected by forms analogous to the dissonances heard in the music of Schoenberg and other modern composers. In both modern music and narrative, the fullness of the fragmentary, the absurd, the alienated, and the grotesquely parodied: all of these features of such art constitute an attempt to formulate—to cherish and render—what endures in us as human, for such destabilizing dissonance becomes an index of the potential for a freed life in the face of the order and "reality" of modern society. The suspension of that order—of its binding myths and conventions as fictions—is achieved in both music and narrative in the modern period by dissonance and its emancipation, which "debunks" the fixity of forms and selves while enacting the possibility of their liberation. "An art that self-consciously debunk[s] its illusory claims to wholeness and self-sufficiency"—Martin Jay writes of Adorno's late view of dissonant, "de-aestheticized" art—is "more capable of negating" the order of society, selves, and forms than one which keeps up the "pretense." Moreover by resisting the "conceptual" imperatives of philosophical analysis, dissonant art more closely provides "a flickering utopian model of what mankind, despite everything, might become."[1]

    The roots of modernist fiction, and even of narrative itself, are to be found in this struggle, through traps of self and society, toward the utopian "realm of heretical freedom." That last phrase is part of Ernst Bloch's effort in "The Comic Hero" to locate the novel's essential origin in the visionary, "idealistic daydream" of Don Quixote; for Bloch, Quixote's struggle to imagine freely is linked to the "visionary hearing" of music as a similar means to make freedom of perception, of "imagination," live again.[2] The modern novel employs dissonance as the means to revive precisely the "dream" of freedom and fiction making for the reader trapped by twentieth-century "reality." Its reader, its often embattled Quixotic characters, and the writer of dissonant fiction experience such a potential liberation through the use of the range of narrative dislocations that expose the spaces between deadnesses in form or language, revealing those "rifts and crevices"—in Adorno's phrase—as areas of freedom for the author's creation and the reader's active entry: cracks made by clashes and renovations in diction, by disorienting and reinvigorating shifts from minimalizing to colossal effects, or by the ironic disintegration and reassembling of character, plot, and structure generally. Such are some of the dissonances—for both writer and reader—which fill the novels of Proust, Mann, Joyce, and other modern novelists.

In Proust the analogy between fiction and Nietzschean dissonance illuminates the "purely musical impressions, non-extensive, entirely original . . . *sine materia*" (I 227–28), which underpin the freed elaboration of consciousness within a "remembrance of things past." The dissonant metaphor reminds us of Proust's movement away from the Schopenhaurian solace that some readers see yielded in the narrative, and toward a Nietzschean process yielding the simultaneous vitality and instability of the novel's intentions and achievement, its vision of aesthetic truth and of characters always unfolding in imagined time—"giants in time"—wavering between lie and "truth," between the metaphor of pure fiction and the metonymy of involuntary memory. Proust's novel is an epic dissonance, confrontative and unstable and fertile for the reader, taking him hostage, his sole escape into a fullness of response echoing Proust's own engagement. Indeed the idea of dissonance likewise illuminates Proust's concern with reading, with opening to perception "musical impressions . . . *sine materia*," not only in Marcel's experience but in the reader's engagement of them; Proust's "composition" of these absences, these fictions with their world encompassing consciousness should become the reader's own "book of his inner being" (III 949).

Similarly, in *Doctor Faustus*, Thomas Mann's dissonant rhetoric intentionally prompts and relies on the reader to implicate himself in

Zeitblom's generous and tragic search for the now incinerated Apollonian. Indeed, Mann's reader must assemble and "compose" the musical play of Zeitblom's and Leverkühn's interlocking and self-disintegrating ironies. In each page of the narrative, a complex sense of simultaneous promise and danger for the reader is to be heard. With its clash between the Nietzschean composer's attempt to transmute hellish agonies into Dionysian delight, and its awed and driven narrator, who is himself a menaced, yearning reader/listener, this Nietzschean, dissonant text questions the very grammar and origins of the modern mode of being conscious, of making claims about existence, of making art. The modern reader (like Zeitblom, our double, our twin, our brother) enters into the freed practice of an abundant, fictive, projective comprehension, yet such a practice engages a potentially agonized destabilizing of what seems to be known, felt, assumed about existence. Like Leverkühn's listener, the reader of dissonant narrative struggles to overcome the absolute anxiety of negation, the consciousness of the end of consciousness. The potentially endless creativity of our engagement mirrors—and is spurred by—an endless questioning, a void, a perception of what perhaps cannot be endured, at the core of darkness.

As we experience this rhetorical and existential dissonance in Mann (as in Conrad), the ground of the perceiver's engagement is established at this zero point of paradox where strategies of negation provide the means of consciousness's survival. This is the ground zero from which other responses may build in the reader, other potential varieties of engagement, for example, the play of selves and worlds yielded when we enter the fiction of Proust and particularly of Joyce: their texts enable us to experience a creative freedom achieved by the challenging, paradoxical, defamiliarizing rhetoric of dissonance. In these same terms, the Nietzschean metaphor of dissonance for fiction's modern strategy also helps us to gauge the "musicality" of Conrad's or of Lawrence's fictiond.

Not merely quasi-musical techniques, but the aim of the dissonant imagination is at work in the "sinister resonance" of Marlow's self- and world-doubting narrative—with its prefiguring of Zeitblom— and in the "Dionysian" tensions of *Women in Love*. Partly as in the Nietzschean "drama" of dissonance, Lawrence's fictions during and after the Great War seek to achieve the resurrection he yearns for in the reader's imagination, a rising to the challenge of affirming not habitual consciousness but a freed and creative Dionysian consciousness in the face of death—indeed the death of conventional narrative itself. With regard to Lawrence's exposing and exposed aim finally that the reader choose the freed comprehension of desire, Mark Schorer's remark about *Women in Love* bears repeating: "no novelist speaks more directly to us, and if we can't hear him, we are, I quite believe, lost."[3]

Finally, with Joyce, in *Ulysses*, the challenge of the Sirens' song of dissonance is most concerted and significant, for in Joyce's play with the Nietzschean dynamics of tragic modernity, he achieves a comic fertility, a masculine mothering—as it is termed—of fictive paradox, parody, and vision. The relevance here of the musical metaphor again does not simply involve the "musical" structures often detected in his work. The metaphor applies, above all, to the reader's engagement of the novel's "dissonance," that is, he is placed in the position of comprehending and navigating among the wealth of destabilizing, discordant fictions constituting language and consciousness. These include fictive selves or "readings" fixed in their disintegrating alienation or their revolt or their fullness of desire, and this wealth of "readings"— of language and fictions here—includes all manner of ordering, of structuring, Freudian, for example, or "scientific" or "mythic." *Ulysses* suspends within the reader's consciousness a complex, contradictory overabundance of fictions, a full fictive "universe" achieved for and by the exercise of the reader's imaginative entry. Both the risk of alienating, fragmenting, anarchic self-dispossession and the great, intrinsic opportunity for freeing, metamorphosizing fantasy are evident in the "dissonant" play of fictions which prompts as well as constitutes the reader's engagement here. The tenor of the dissonant metaphor is suggested, somewhat deceptively, by Joyce's adolescent aphorism that a modern text—as a test of the reader's consciousness—is "not to be criticized, but to be faced and lived." The mature Joyce has transfigured these claims of alienated defiance, so that he offers the reader an opportunity to achieve what is a Dionysian affirmation of consciousness, its superfluity of fictions designed indeed to challenge the reader to engage the processes of a freed consciousness.

A passage I examined in chapter 7 from the "Sirens" episode of *Ulysses* further clarifies that challenge, and I return to it in order again to distinguish between, on the one hand, "musical structure" or a "prose music" and, on the other hand, the rhetorical process and aim of the modern, dissonant text. Here is Bloom's perception of the high, tenor note Simon sings in the aria "M'appari":

—Come!

It soared, a bird, it held its flight, a swift pure cry, come, don't spin it out too long long breath he breath long life, soaring high, high resplendent, aflame, crowned, high in the effulgence symbolistic, high, of the ethereal bosom, high, of the high vast irradiation everywhere all soaring all around about the all, the endlessnessnessness.

—To me!

Siopold! (226–27)

That the passage presents and parodies a self-consciously musical prose is not my point here; the more profound function of the passage is to confront the reader with the implications of the musical "image" for the perceiver. Bloom's experience is enclosed within a structure of comedy and negation which both victimizes and enhances his perceptions. Joyce's aim is to place the reader himself in the crucial position of perceiving and judging how the freed vitality of consciousness endures within the "endless" negations or creative fictionality of this dissonant form. Bloom's creative identification with the operatic character Lionel and the singer Simon ("Siopold!") offers two crucial understandings for the reader. First, it is not only the singer contained in Leopold: it is the possible future of Stephen. It is the Dionysian dance of existence ever aware of brilliant formal Apollo shaping, instructing, calling out the patterns; "greekjew meets jewgreek," indeed. Here we see enacted Joyce's play and acceptance of both the Hellenic and the Hebraic impulses in his art. The process he imagines in Bloom tied to his mast here is, above all, a comically affirming concept of the exfoliating possible selves in the midst of the flux of life (though where I see modernist flux, other critics—as I have noted—see modernist detritus). And this notion of Bloom's "process" brings us to the second key import of the passage: Bloom's response as a perceiver offers us an image for the reader's creative engagement of the strategy of Dionysian dissonance in *Ulysses*. Our reading of the text—an exercise of freed consciousness on which the work's value depends—is a version of Bloom's joyous, furtive yet open, fertilely self-creative involvement with music above, only aware of the distortion, the dispossessing imaginative risk of self, the fictive fullness within negation which are involved in the activity of reading and our response: Siopold!

The crucial understanding conveyed by the critical metaphor of dissonance is then that a novel like *Ulysses*, *Remembrance of Things Past*, or *Doctor Faustus* draws the reader into a radical relationship to fiction, whether emphasizing the tragic desperation of modernity's situation or the comic plentitude which yet can infuse the menaced and difficult process of perception. The rhetorical strategy of the modern novel aims to resurrect meaning in the face of its disappearance amid the entrapping ruin of the modern world. Such is the ambition of these novelists: to evoke from the reader a critical practice of imaginative consciousness, a self-challenging and creative process of perception and judgment which constitutes the freed activity of reading.

The greatness of their achievement is, as the wisdom resonating in these risk-taking texts would suggest, profoundly paradoxical. A novel like *Doctor Faustus* disintegrates the ordering priorities and structures of consciousness in the reader, and simultaneously its casting into doubt makes possible a liberation of consciousness or, better, of language itself as a struggle, a process, of continual, ambiguous possibility, of fictive becoming. In part, this Nietzschean paradox in the modern novel's achievement exerts an agonizing pressure for imaginative renewal on the reader's consciousness. Its negations ever more pressingly speak out: "You must change your life." The significance of this paradox is, finally, that the modern novel stirs in the reader a radical exercise of imaginative power which echoes yet transfigures the alienated skepticism that modern fiction simultaneously imagines.

The nature of that imaginative power is illuminated, as we have seen, by the ideas of Theodor Adorno, which expose the simultaneously demystifying and reconstructive strategy essential to the metaphor of dissonance in modern fiction. Such a conception is explored also by contemporary theories like Barthes's conception of the creative "pleasure" of reading in the workshop of the text or Derrida's sense that writing's function should be to resist the totalizing structures of contemporary Western experience; such resistance is essentially an access to freedom of language and imagination. When divested of the Derridian commitment to (self-dis)play, this point is implicit in the notion of reading as a process which moves away from the structuring and representation of empirical or of metaphysical "reality," into the search of a freed consciousness for imaginative meaning.

The risk and experience of the vanished self as the reader engages the self-challenging form of modern fiction leads him to activate the potential in language and consciousness to work through to the center of their revolutionary creativity. This conception is suggested, too, by Robert M. Adams' exploration of "strains of discord" in modern literature, and in earlier, theoretical formulations of modernism from Sartre to Suzanne Langer. It is also clear in Frank Kermode's mention of the "discoveries of dissonance" that the reader seeks in modern fiction.[4] In *The Sense of An Ending*, Kermode contrasts that search with the false solace provided by "easier" fictions and conceptions of fiction that deny the "harder truths" and struggle which the temporal, dissonant form of the modern novel reveals. In a critique of Joseph Frank's early New Critical notion of spatial form and its containment of modern literature's self-reflexive multiplicity, Kermode writes that one of the critic's duties is

> to abandon ways of speaking which on the one hand obscure the true nature of our fictions—by confusing them with myths, by rendering spatial what is essentially temporal—and on the other obscure our sense of reality by suggesting that fictions represent some kind of surrender or false consolation. The critical issue, given the perpetual assumption of crisis, is no less than the justification of ideas of order.[5]

Given the simultaneously demystifying and reconstructive vision which challenges us in the novels of Conrad, Mann, Proust, Lawrence and Joyce, the reader engages and seeks to develop the paradoxical and risk-taking freedom, fertility, and plentitude of a fiction-generating consciousness.

Such terms—"risk" or "freedom" or "consciousness" itself, all describing the process of reading the modern, dissonant novel—derive in part from the tradition I discussed of nineteenth- and earlier twentieth-century thought, yet it is clear that these terms have also been absorbed into later twentieth-century cultural institutions and practice, just as Marxist, Freudian, formalist, feminist, deconstructive, or technological terms become the usurped tools of academic, institutional authority. A necessary anxiety about this usurpation can yield in criticism a struggling allusiveness, teetering between revolt and capitulation. The anxiety of critical discourse offers a darkened mirror for the creative anxiety of reading modern fiction.

A similar destabilizing "play" of dissonance confronts the reader of twentieth-century poetry, and the distinction can be illuminating between poetic and narrative applications of the musical analogy.

For example, Rilke's creation of the musical metaphor—in "To Music," in the *Duino Elegies*, in the *Sonnets to Orpheus*—develops the paradoxical image of Dionysian disintegration to be found also in his sonnet "on the torso of Apollo." In "To Music," for instance, Rilke's evocation of music as the "breathing of statues" renders his yearning for a liberation of self, of consciousness, and of a potential in language itself: Music is "language where all language / ends."[6] The tension in the poet's exploration of that paradox on the edge of silence constitutes a profound cry of dissonance in modern lyric. In the perspective of such dissonance, negation—the "no longer habitable"—becomes a sign of inner perception, of music's enduring power, for Rilke's recurrent lyric cries to the unseizable and the uninhabitable recognize precisely the uninhabitability of all presence, in the present time. Simultaneously, however, his is a joyous cry paradoxically discovering (as noted by Walter Strauss and other commentators)[7] a song-language which—charged by its alienation from the present—is full of the imagining of an alternative, meaningful time, of the "reality" evoked by the *Sonnets to Orpheus*. Sonnet 13, for example, imagines a potentiality beyond the absence of meaning in our time and place: "True singing is a different breath, about / nothing. A gust inside the god. A wind."[8] Yeats and Eliot in the same years after the First World War project similar paradoxes of alienated song in which the fragmentary surviving spirit must struggle to "sing / for every tatter in its mortal dress."[9] The tragic fullness of modernist dissonance is apparent here in "Sailing to Byzantium" as in much of Yeats's work in this period, and it also clearly suffuses Eliot's alternatively Wagnerian and Nietzschean *The Wasteland* and later his *Four Quartets*.[10]

Finally, it is modern fiction's aim and struggle to imagine fully the fictive world to which the lyric cry of modernist poetry testifies. The modern novel in analogous yet quite different ways transforms its structures and capabilities, for fiction is rooted above all in the world encompassing and confronting fictive histories of Quixote, of epics both serious and mocking, especially mock. The modern descendents of Quixote take up the Nietzschean task and insight of Dionysian dissonance, compounded of alienation and the human struggle towards critical and imaginative freedom. The tragic imprisonment in alienated deprivation is where each of the novelists we are exploring begins, indeed where Conrad and Mann reveal consciousness to be in desperate struggle, and the possibility of affirming the struggle in all its fullness—as well as the liberating, critical reach through it—is imagined with increasing ambition by them, by Proust, Joyce, and other modern novelists.

These novelists offer the reader forms created to resuscitate the vital tension within and between language and imagination in an alienated, entrapping time and culture. Dissonant novels as different as *Ulysses* and *Doctor Faustus* assume this critical, creative risk and participation. That is what the musical paradigm in Rousseau, Beethoven, and above all in Nietzsche's thought enables us to understand: how the reader of the modern novel places himself at—and becomes—the focus of modern fiction and its imaginative process. The reader of *Doctor Faustus* imagines the agony of witness before Apollo destroyed; the reader of *Ulysses* imagines the energy of ceaseless Dionysus. By offering an understanding of the reader's opportunity in the face of the modern novel's self-disintegrating form, the dissonant musical metaphor enables us to imagine a radical bridge between the ethics and aesthetics of modern fiction. Nietzsche shows us that the perception of dissonance liberates the fiction-generating process, engendered in revolt within the mire and empire of contingent, habitual "consciousness."

The modern reader's challenging task—central to the profound and distinguishing aim of the novel earlier in the twentieth century—is to engage, with a creative, destabilized, fertile, and anxious delight, fiction's revolutionary and encompassing opening-up of the processes of language, fantasy, and perception. The depth and energy of the reader's self-challenging response—his exploration of the elemental, fiction generating process within the negations Proust, Mann, or Joyce present—constitute a crucial, liberating test of consciousness amid the ambiguous subversions and ironic abundance of dissonant narrative. Reading modern, dissonant fiction is, then, an activity by which the reader discovers and explores the freed capability of consciousness. To adapt Ortega y Gasset's Nietzschean phrase,[11] the reader becomes the novelist of the fictive selves to be imagined, of the fictive worlds to be constructed, finally of himself and his world comprehended now in the perspective—or, better, the process—of imaginative becoming.

Notes

Chapter 1. A Sinister Resonance

1. Geoffrey Hartman, *Criticism in the Wilderness: The Study of Literature Today* (New Haven: Yale University Press, 1 980), p. 26.

2. George Steiner, *Language and Silence* (London: Faber and Faber, 1967), pp. 62–63.

3. René Welleck and Austin Warren, *Theory of Literature* (New York: Harcourt Brace and World, 1956), p. 129.

4. Joseph Conrad, *Youth and Two Other Stories* (Garden City, N.Y.: Doubleday, Page and Co., 1927), p. xi.

5. Mark Schorer, *The World We Imagine: Selected Essays* (New York: Farrar, Straus and Giroux, 1968), p. 19.

6. Conrad, *Youth*, p. 160.

7. Joseph Conrad, *The Nigger of the 'Narcissus'* (Garden City, N.Y.: Doubleday, Page and Co., 1924), pp. xiii–xiv.

8. Conrad, *Youth*, pp. 113–14.

9. Theodor Adorno, *Introduction to the Sociology of Music*, trans. E. B. Ashton (New York: Seabury Press, 1976), pp. 50–51.

10. Theodor Adorno, *Philosophy of Modern Music*, trans. Anne Mitchell and Wesley Bloomster (New York: Seabury Press, 1973), p. 86.

11. Ibid.

12. Theodor Adorno, *Minima Moralia: Reflections from Damaged Life,* trans. E. F. N. Sephcott (London: NLB, 1974), p. 247.

13. See Bloch's and Adorno's joint interview in Ernst Bloch, *The Utopian Function of Art and Literature: Selected Essays*, trans. Jack Zipes and Frank Mecklenburg (Cambridge: MIT Press, 1988), pp. 1–17.

14. Ernst Bloch, *Philosophy of Music*, trans. Peter Palmer (Cambridge: Cambridge University Press, 1985), p. 124.

15. Ibid., pp. 130–31.

16. Ibid., p. 133
17. Ibid., p. 135.
18. Joseph Conrad, *Notes on Life and Literature* (Garden City, N.Y.: Doubleday, Page and Co., 1925), p. 13.
19. Ibid., pp. 13–14.
20. Chris Norris, "Utopian Deconstruction: Ernst Bloch, Paul de Man and the Politics of Music," *Paragraph* 11:1 (March 1988): p. 41.
21. Peter Osborne, "Adorno and the Metaphysics of Modernism: The Problem of 'Postmodern' Art," in *The Problems of Modernity: Adorno and Benjamin*, ed. Andrew Benjamin (London: Routledge and Kegan Paul, 1989), p. 37.
22. Friederich Nietzsche, *Basic Writings of Friederich Nietzsche*, trans. Walter Kaufmann (New York: Modern Library, 1968), p. 729.
23. Claude Lévesque, "Dissonance," in *Études Françaises* 17 (3–4): (October 1981): 60, and "Language to the Limit," in *Nietzsche and the Rhetoric of Nihilism,* eds. Tom Darby, Bela Egyed, and Ben Jones (Ottawa: Carleton University Press, 1989), p. 52.
24. Nietzsche, *Basic Writings*, p. 710.
25. See John Burt Foster, *Heirs to Dionysus: A Nietzschean Current in Literary Modernism* (Princeton: Princeton University Press, 1981), and Philip Weinstein, *The Semantics of Desire: Changing Modes of Identity from Dickens to Joyce* (Princeton: Princeton University Press, 1984).
26. Maurice Blanchot, *The Sirens' Song*, trans. Sacha Rabinovitch (Bloomington: Indiana University Press, 1982), p. 59.
27. Steiner, *Language and Silence*, pp. 62–63, 66.
28. Ihab Hassan, *The Dismemberment of Orpheus: Towards a Post-modern Literature* (New York: Oxford University Press, 1971).
29. Calvin S. Brown, *Music and Literature: A Comparison of the Arts* (Athens: University of Georgia Press, 1948).
30. Ezra Pound, "M. James Joyce et Pécuchet" in *Polite Essays* (New York: Books for Libraries Press, 1937).
31. Alex Aronson, *Music and the Novel: A Study in Twentieth Century Fiction* (Totowa, N.J.: Rowman and Littlefield, 1980).
32. Carl Dahlhaus, *Schoenberg and the New Music*, trans. Derrick Puffett and Alfred Clayton (New York: Cambridge University Press, 1987), p. 27.
33. Françoise Meltzer, *Salome and the Dance of Writing* (Chicago: University of Chicago Press, 1987).
34. Wassily Kandinsky and Arnold Schoenberg, *Arnold Schoenberg-Wassily Kandinsky: Letters, Pictures and Documents,* trans. John C. Crawford (London: Faber and Faber, 1984), p. 21.
35. See Carl Schorske, *Fin-de Siècle Vienna: Politics and Culture* (New York: Knopf, 1980), and Frederick Karl, *Modern and Modernism* (New York: Atheneum, 1988).
36. Robert P. Morgan, "Secret Languages: The Roots of Musical Modernism," in *Modernism: Challenges and Perspectives* eds. M. Chefdor, K. Quinones, and A. Wachtel (Urbana: University of Illinois Press, 1986), p. 36.

37. Carl Dahlhaus, *Between Romanticism and Modernism: Four Studies in the Music of the Later Nineteenth Century*, trans. Mary Whittall (Berkeley: University of California Press, 1980), p. 8.

38. Erich Heller, *The Disinherited Mind* (Cleveland: World Publishing Co., 1959), p. 265.

Chapter 2. Early Romantic Ideas of Music

1. M. H. Abrams, *The Mirror and the Lamp* (New York: W. W. Norton, 1953), p. 53 ff.

2. Johann Wolfgang Goethe, *Faust*, trans. Louis MacNeice (New York: Oxford University Press, 1960), p. 21.

3. Friederich Nietzsche, *Portable Nietzsche*, trans. Walter Kaufmann (New York: Modern Library, 1968), p. 554.

4. Jean-Jacques Rousseau, *The Reveries of a Solitary*, trans. J. B. Fletcher (New York: Burt Franklin, 1971), p. 113.

5. See Jacques Derrida, *Of Grammatology*, trans. G. Chakravorty Spivak (Baltimore: Johns Hopkins University Press, 1977), p. 199; Paul de Man, *Blindness and Insight* (New Haven: Yale University Press, 1971), pp. 128–32; also, Paul de Man, *Allegories of Reading* (New Haven: Yale University Press, 1979), p. 270; as well, there is the useful summary in Chris Norris, *Deconstructionism: Theory and Practice* (New York: Methuen, 1982), p. 34–35.

6. Jean-Jacques Rousseau, *Essay on the Origin of Languages*, trans. John H. Moran and Alexander Gode (Chicago: University of Chicago Press, 1966), p. 64.

7. Norris, *Deconstructionism*, p. 107.

8. Rousseau, *Reveries*, p. 116.

9. Leo Schrade, *Beethoven in France: The Growth of an Idea* (New Haven: Yale University Press, 1942), p. 45.

10. Quoted in Erich Heller, *The Artist's Journey into the Interior* (New York: Vintage, 1968), p. 129.

11. Thomas Mann, *Doctor Faustus*, trans. H. T. Lowe-Porter (New York: Modern Library, 1948), p. 53. All further references in the text are to this edition.

12. Schrade, *Beethoven*, p. 40.

13. Marcel Proust, *Remembrance of Things Past*, trans. C. K. Scott Moncrieff and Terence Kilmartin (New York: Random House, 1981), Vol. III, p. 943. All further references in the text are to this edition.

14. Theodor Adorno, *Aesthetic Theory*, trans. C. Lenhardt (London: Routledge and Kegan Paul, 1984), p. 196.

15. Ferruccio Busoni, *The Essence of Music and Other Essays*, trans. Rosamond Ley (New York: Dover, 1965), p. 130.

16. Adorno, *Philosophy of Modern Music*, p. 198.

17. Ludwig van Beethoven, *Piano Sonatas*, Urtext edition (Berlin: Henle, 1960), p. 233.

18. J. W. N. Sullivan, *Beethoven: His Spiritual Development* (New York: Vintage, 1960), pp. 136–40.

19. Leo Schrade, *Tragedy in the Art of Music* (Cambridge: Harvard University Press, 1964), pp. 118–19, 129.

20. Bloch, *Philosophy of Music*, p. 34.

21. Wilfrid Mellers, *Caliban Reborn: Renewal in Twentieth Century Music* (New York: Harper and Row, 1967), p. 32.

22. Ibid., pp. 181–82.

23. Maynard Solomon, *Beethoven* (New York: Schirmer, 1977), pp. 315–16.

24. Joseph Kerman, *Contemplating Music: Challenges to Musicology* (Cambridge: Harvard University Press, 1985), p. 111.

25. Leonard B. Meyer, *Music, the Arts, and Ideas* (Chicago: University of Chicago Press, 1967).

26. Charles Rosen, *Arnold Schoenberg* (New York: Viking, 1975), p. 60.

27. E. M. Forster, *Howards End* (New York: Knopf, 1921), p. 34.

28. D. H. Lawrence, *Aaron' s Rod*, (1922; reprinted New York: Penguin, 1976), p. 202.

29. Adorno, *Sociology of Music*, p. 209.

30. Ibid., pp. 209, 214.

31. Frederic Jameson, "Introduction" to Jacques Attali, *Noise* (Minneapolis: University of Minnesota Press, 1985), p. ix.

32. Attali, *Noise*, pp. 30–31.

33. See, for example, Terry Eagleton, *The Ideology of the Aesthetic* (Oxford: Basil Blackwell, 1990), pp. 361–63; and Frederic Jameson, *The Syntax of History*, vol. II of *Ideologies of Theory* (Minneapolis: University of Minnesota Press, 1988), p. 144.

34. Adorno, *Aesthetic Theory*, p. 22.

35. Adorno, *Sociology of Music*, p. 214.

36. Selden Rodman, *The Heart of Beethoven* (New York: Shorewood, 1962), p. 109.

37. Ibid., p. 38.

38. Roland Barthes, "Musica Practica," in *Image/Music/Text*, trans. Stephen Heath (New York: Hill and Wang, 1977), p. 153.

39. Roland Barthes, *S/Z*, trans. Richard Miller (New York: Hill and Wang, 1974), pp. 30, 42. See also Bakhtin's study of Dostoyevsky's poetics.

Chapter 3. Literature and Music in the Nineteenth Century

1. Thomas Mann, *Essays of Three Decades*, trans. H. T. Lowe-Porter (New York: Knopf, 1965), p. 396.

2. Arthur Schopenhauer, *Schopenhauer: Selections*, ed. and trans. D. H. Parker (New York: Scribner's, 1956), pp. 98–99.

Notes

3. Mann, *Essays*, p. 410.

4. A. G. Lehmann, *The Symbolist Aesthetic in France* (Oxford: Basil Blackwell, 1968), pp. 59, 64.

5. Schopenhauer, *Selections*, pp. 177–82.

6. Thomas Mann, *Buddenbrooks*, trans. H. T. Lowe-Porter (1924; reprint New York: Knopf, 1964).

7. Mann, *Essays*, p. 386.

8. See Robert Schumann, "Davidsbündlerblatter," in *Source Readings in Music History: The Romantic Era*, ed. Oliver Strunk (New York: W. W. Norton, 1965).

9. Quoted in Martin Turnell, *Baudelaire: A Study of His Poetry* (London: Hamish Hamilton, 1953), p. 118.

10. Blanchot, *The Sirens' Song*, pp. 64–65.

11. Ibid., p. 59.

12. Ibid., p. 102.

13. Charles Baudelaire, *The Flowers of Evil*, rev. ed., eds. M. and J. Matthews (Norfolk: New Directions, 1963), pp. 85–86.

14. Ibid., p. 2.

15. Miriam Allott, ed., *Novelists on the Novel* (New York: Columbia University Press, 1959), p. 240.

16. Gustave Flaubert, *Madame Bovary,* trans. Paul de Man (New York: W. W. Norton, 1965), p. 107

17. Ibid., p. 138.

18. Stéphane Mallarmé, "Music and Literature," trans. Bradford Cook, in *Modern Continental Literary Criticism*, ed. O. B. Hardison (New York: Appleton Century Crofts, 1962), pp. 176–78.

19. Stéphane Mallarmé, *Selected Poetry and Prose*, selected and edited by Mary Ann Caws (New York: New Directions, 1982), pp. 103ff .

20. Paul Verlaine, "Ars Poetica," in *An Anthology of French Poetry from Nerval to Valery*, ed. Angel Flores (Garden City, N.Y.: Doubleday, 1958), p. 99.

21. Lehmann, *The Symbolist Aesthetic*, p. 210 ff.

22. Mallarmé, "Music and Literature," p. 178.

23. Jean-Pol Madou, "Langue, Mythe, musique: Rousseau, Nietzsche, Mallarmé, Lévi-Strauss," in *Littérature et Musique*, ed. Raphael Celis (Bruxelles: Facultes universitaires Saint Louis, 1982), pp. 88–89.

24. Meltzer, *Salome and the Dance of Writing*, pp. 45–46.

25. Walter Pater, *Studies in the Rennaisance* (Cleveland: World Publishing Co., 1961), p. 132.

26. Ibid., p. 222.

27. Ibid., p. 123.

28. William Butler Yeats, *Autobiographies* (New York: Collier, 1965), p. 201.

29. Mann, *Essays*, pp. 350–51.

30. Lehmann, *The Symbolist Aesthetic*, p. 230.

31. Steven Paul Scher, "Literature and Music," in *Interrelations of Literature*, eds. Jean-Pierre Barricelli and Joseph Gibaldi (New York: MLA, 1982); and John Louis DiGaetani, *Wagner and the Modern British Novel* (Rutherford, N.J.: Fairleigh Dickinson University Press, 1978).

32. See James Joyce, "Ibsen's New Drama" in *The Critical Writings of James Joyce*, eds. Ellsworth Mason and Richard Ellmann (New York: Viking, 1959).

33. Thomas Mann, "Sufferings and Greatness of Richard Wagner" in *Essays*.

34. Quoted in Turnell, *Baudelaire*, p. 118.

35. Lehmann, *The Symbolist Aesthetic*, p. 228.

36. Richard Wagner, "The Art-Work of the Future," in *Source Readings*, ed. Oliver Strunk, p. 136.

37. Nietzsche, "The Case of Wagner" in *Basic Writings*, p. 621.

38. Joseph Kerman, *Opera as Drama*, rev. ed. (Berkeley: University of California Press, 1988).

39. Bloch, *Philosophy of Music*, p. 62.

40. Adorno, *Sociology of Music*, pp. 50–51.

Chapter 4. Music and the Modern Imagination

1. Nietzsche, *Portable Nietzsche*, p. 669.

2. Ibid., pp. 666–70.

3. Ibid., p. 667; Nietzsche, *Basic Writings*, p. 22.

4. Nietzsche, *Portable Nietzsche*, pp. 667, 670.

5. Adorno, *Sociology of Music*, pp. 50–51.

6. Nietzsche, *Basic Writings*, pp. 17 ff., and *Portable Nietzsche*, pp. 670, 677.

7. Jacques Derrida, *Spurs: Nietzsche's Styles*, trans. Barbara Harlow (Chicago: University of Chicago Press, 1979), pp. 43–45.

8. Nietzsche, *Portable Nietzsche*, pp. 99–100

9. David S. Allison, ed., "Introduction," *The New Nietzsche: Contemporary Styles in Interpretation* (New York: Dell, 1977), p. xx.

10. Gilles Deleuze, "Active and Reactive," in *The New Nietzsche*, ed. Allison, pp. 80 ff.

11. Nietzsche, *Portable Nietzsche*, pp. 97–98.

12. Derrida, *Spurs*, p. 127.

13. De Man, *Allegories of Reading*, pp. 199–201.

14. Nietzsche, *Basic Writings*, p. 710.

15. De Man, *Blindness and Insight*, p. 64.

16. Ibid., pp. 47–48.

17. Ibid., p. 162.

18. Nietzsche, *Portable Nietzsche*, pp. 46–47.

Notes

19. Harold Bloom, *Wallace Stevens: The Poems of Our Climate* (Ithaca: Cornell University Press, 1977), p. 393.

20. Jonathan Arac, "Aesthetics, Rhetoric, History: Paul de Man and the American Use of Nietzsche," in *Why Nietzsche Now?* ed. Daniel O'Hara (Bloomington: Indiana University Press, 1985), p. 428.

21. Heller, *Artist's Journey*, pp. 194–98.

22. Nietzsche, *Basic Writings*, p. 751.

23. Nietzsche, *The Birth of Tragedy*, Sections 5–7, in *Basic Writings*, particularly pp. 59–60.

24. Arthur C. Danto, *Nietzsche as Philosopher* (New York: Macmillan, 1965), pp. 227–28.

25. See Sarah Kofman, "Metaphor, Symbol, Metamorphosis," in *The New Nietzsche*, ed. Allison, p. 204.

26. Nietzsche, *Basic Writings*, p. 141.

27. Ibid., p. 142.

28. Dahlhaus, *Between Romanticism and Modernism*, p. 106–19.

29. Ibid., p. 20.

30. Nietzsche, *Basic Writings*, p. 27.

31. Charles Altieri, "Ecce Homo: Narcissism, Power, Pathos, and the Status of Autobiographical Representation," in *Why Nietzsche Now?* ed. Daniel O'Hara, (Bloomington, Indiana University Press, 1985), p. 406. Alexander Nehamas, *Nietzsche: Life as Literature* (Cambridge: Harvard University Press, 1985).

32. Michael Foucault, *Language/Countermemory/Practice*, trans. Donald F. Bouchard and Sherry Simon (Ithaca: Cornell University Press, 1977), p. 142.

33. Kathleen Higgins, *Nietzsche's Zarathustra* (Philadelphia: Temple University Press, 1987), p. 183.

34. Ibid., p. 184.

35. Pierre Klossowski, "Nietzsche's Experience of the Eternal Return," in Allison, *The New Nietzsche*, p. 114.

36. Lévesque, "Language to the Limit," p. 49.

37. See particularly Nietzsche, *Basic Writings*, p. 489.

38. D. H. Lawrence, *Apocalypse*, (1931; reprinted New York: Penguin, 1976), p. 53.

39. Ibid., pp. 125–26.

40. Nietzsche, *Portable Nietzsche*, p. 185.

41. D. H. Lawrence, *The Man Who Died*, (1928; reprinted New York: Vintage, 1953), p. 188.

42. Ibid., p. 202.

43. Ibid., p. 211.

44. Blanchot, *The Sirens' Song*, pp. 178–79.

45. Lévesque, "Language to the Limit," p. 53.

46. Arnold Schoenberg, *String Quartet, Opus 10* (New York: Schirmer, 1939).

47. Rosen, *Schoenberg*, pp. 20–21.

48. Arnold Schoenberg, *Style and Idea*, trans. Leonard Stein (New York: Philosophical Library, 1950), p. 71.

49. Dahlhaus, *Schoenberg*, p. 120; and Rosen, *Schoenberg,* p. 63.

50. Anton Webern, *The Path to the New Music* (New York: Presser, 1963).

51. Stanley Cavell, *Must We Mean What We Say?* (Cambridge: Cambridge University Press, 1976), p. 206.

52. Adorno, *Philosophy of Modern Music*, p. 212.

53. Ibid., p. 133.

54. Theodor Adorno, *Prisms*, trans. Samuel and Shierry Weber (Cambridge: MIT Press, 1981), p . 150.

55. Jean-Francois Lyotard, "Several Silences," in *Driftworks*, trans. Roger McKeon (New York: Columbia University Press, 1984); John Anderson Winn, Unsuspected Eloquence (New Haven: Yale University Press, 1981) pp. 336–38;and John Shepard et al., *Whose Music? A Sociology of Musical Languages* (New Brunswick, N.J.: Transaction Books, 1977).

56. Lyotard, "Several Silences," pp. 105–6.

57. Ibid., pp. 99,106.

58. Ibid., pp. 108–9.

59. Dahlhaus, *Schoenberg*, pp. 276–77; Arthur Kroker and David Cook, *The Postmodern Scene: Excremental Culture and Hyper-Aesthetics* (New York: St. Martin's Press, 1988), p. 258.

60. Arnold Schoenberg, *Moses und Aron: Oper in drei Akten* (New York: Schott Music Corp., 1958), p. 540.

Chapter 5. The Dissonant Aesthetic in Continental Fiction

1. Franz Kafka, *The Penal Colony: Stories and Short Pieces*, trans. Willa and Edwin Muir (New York: Schocken, 1948), p. 173.

2. Albert Camus, *The Myth of Sisyphus and Other Essays*, trans. by Richard Howard (New York: Vintage, 1960), p. 102.

3. Kafka, *The Penal Colony*, p. 121.

4. Hermann Broch, *Death of Virgil*, trans. Jean Starr Untermeyer (New York: Pantheon, 1945).

5. See, for an early statement of of this conception, Charles Fiedelson, *Symbolism and American Literature* (Chicago: University of Chicago Press, 1953), p. 189; André Gide, *The Counterfeiters*, trans. Dorothy Bussy (New York: Knopf, 1951).

6. Albert Guerard, *André Gide* (Cambridge: Harvard University Press, 1951), pp. 164 –65.

7. See George Schoolfield, *The Figure of the Musician in German Literature* (Chapel Hill: University of North Carolina Press, 1956), pp. 192–93; Herman Hesse, *Steppenwolf*,

trans. Basil Creighton (New York: Holt, Rinehart, Winston, 1961) and *The Glass Bead Game*, trans. Richard and Clara Winston (New York: Holt, Rinehart, Winston, 1969).

8. Mann, *Essays*, p. 396.

9. All references in the text are to the Montcrieff-Kilmartin translation cited in Chapter 1.

10. Samuel Beckett, *Proust* (New York: Grove Press, 1957), pp. 70–71.

11. Edmund Wilson, *Axel's Castle* (New York: Scribner's, 1930), p. 164.

12. Georges Piroué, *Proust et la musique du devenir* (Paris: Editions Denoel, 1960), p. 166.

13. Marcel Proust, *À la recherche du temps perdu*, vol. III, Pléiade edition, ed. Clarac and Ferre (Bruges: Gallimard, 1954), p. 880.

14. Gilles Deleuze, *Proust and Signs*, trans. Richard Howard (New York: George Braziller, 1972), pp. 58–59.

15. Jean-Jacques Nattiez, *Proust as Musician*, trans. Derrick Puffett (New York: Cambridge University Press, 1989), pp. 10, 32.

16. Ibid., p. 89.

17. Gerard Genette, "Time and Narrative in *À la recherche du temps perdu*," in *Marcel Proust: Modern Critical Views*, ed. Harold Bloom (New York: Chelsea House, 1987), p. 163.

18. Deleuze, *Proust and Signs*, pp. 166–67; de Man, *Allegories of Reading*, pp. 72, 78.

19. Walter Benjamin, *Illuminations*, trans. Harry Zohn (New York: Harcourt Brace Jovanovich, 1968), pp. 205–6.

20. Nattiez, *Proust as Musician*, p. 36.

21. Ibid., p. 75.

22. Genette, "Time and Narrative," p. 163.

23. Ranier Maria Rilke, *Selected Poetry of Rainer Maria Rilke*, trans. Stephen Mitchell (New York: Vintage, 1984), p. 191.

24. Benjamin, *Illuminations*, p. 212.

25. Leo Bersani, "Proust and the Art of Incompletion," in *Aspects of Narrative*, ed. J. Hillis Miller (New Haven: Yale University Press, 1977), p. 175.

26. Adorno, *Prisms*, p. 181.

27. *Ibid.*, p. 183.

Chapter 6. The Ethic of Dissonance

1. Mann, *Essays*, pp. 309–10.

2. Roger Shattuck, "The Devil's Dance: Stravinsky's Corporeal Imagination," in *The Innocent Eye* (New York: Farrar Strauss Giroux, 1984), p. 268; see also, Winn, *Unsuspected Eloquence*, pp. 336–38.

3. Adorno, *Philosophy of Modern Music*, p. 212.

4. Ibid., p. 191.

5. See Carl Dahlhaus, "Fiktive Zwölftonmusic: Thomas Mann und Theodor W. Adorno," in *Deutsche Akademie für Sprache und Dichtung*, Darmstadt Jarbuch 1, 1982; and Gunilla Bergsten, *Thomas Mann's Doctor Faustus* (Chicago: University of Chicago Press, 1969).

6. Thomas Mann, *The Story of A Novel*, trans. H. T. Lowe-Porter (New York: Knopf, 1961), p. 43.

7. Patrick Carnegy, *Faust as Musician: A Study of Thomas Mann's Novel Doctor Faustus* (New York: New Directions, 1973).

8. Schoenberg, *Style and Idea*, p. 142.

9. Mann, *Essays*, p. 386.

10. Stanley Corngold, "Mann as a Reader of Nietzsche," in *The Fate of the Self: German Writers and French Theory* (New York: Columbia University Press, 1986), p. 156.

11. Ibid., p. 146.

12. Ibid., p. 159.

13. Ibid., p. 155.

14. Ibid., p. 159.

15. Thomas Mann, *Death in Venice and Seven Other Stories*, trans. Kenneth Burke (New York: Random House, 1936), p. 26.

16. Ibid., p. 34.

17. Ibid., p. 40.

18. Ibid., p. 70.

19. Ibid., p. 66–68.

20. Ibid., p. 75.

21. Thomas Mann, *The Magic Mountain*, trans. H. T. Lowe-Porter (New York: Modern Library, 1952), p. 721.

22. See Alexander Nehamas, "Nietzsche in *The Magic Mountain*," in *Modern Critical Interpretations of Thomas Mann's The Magic Mountain*, ed. Harold Bloom (New York: Chelsea House, 1986).

23. Mann, *The Magic Mountain*, p. 652.

24. Ibid., pp. 652–53.

25. Heller, *Artist's Journey*, pp. 194 ff.

26. Erich Heller, *In the Age of Prose* (New York: Cambridge University Press, 1984), p. 148.

27. Erich Heller, *The Ironic German* (Boston: Little Brown, 1958), p. 25.

28. Susan van Rohn Scall, "Unending Apocalypse: The Crisis in Musical Narrative in Mann's *Doktor Faustus*," in *Germanic Review* 65:1 (Winter 1990): p. 30.

29. Ibid., p. 31.

30. Heller, *The Ironic German*, pp. 24–25.

31. William M. Honsa Jr., "Parody and Narrator in Thomas Mann's *Doctor Faustus*, in *Thomas Mann: Modern Critical Views*, ed. Harold Bloom (New York: Chelsea House, 1986), p. 223.

Chapter 7. Music and Modern British Fiction

1. See particularly E. M. Forster, *Aspects of the Novel* (New York: Harcourt Brace, 1954), p. 169.

2. Alan Wilde, *Art and Order: A Study of E. M. Forster* (New York: New York University Press, 1964) and *Horizons of Assent: Modernism, Postmodernism, and the Ironic Imagination* (Philadelphia: University of Pennsylvania Press, 1987).

3. Gerald Levin, "The Musical Style of *The Waves*," in *Journal of Narrative Technique* 13 (Fall 1983); Virginia Woolf, *The Waves* (New York: Harcourt Brace, 1931).

4. Virginia Woolf, *Mrs. Dalloway* (New York: Harcourt, Brace, 1925).

5. D. H. Lawrence, *Phoenix II* (New York: Penguin, 1978), p. 276; *Women in Love*, 1920; reprint New York: Penguin, 1982).

6. Weinstein, *The Semantics of Desire*, p. 287.

7. Leo Bersani, *A Future for Astynanax: Character and Desire in Literature* (Boston: Little Brown, 1976), pp. 184–85.

8. Robert Langbaum, *The Mysteries of Identity: A Theme in Modern Literature* (New York: Oxford University Press, 1977), Part II, particularly chapter 10.

9. Weinstein, *The Semantics of Desire*, p. 287.

10. Thomas Flanagan, "Yeats, Joyce, and the Matter of Ireland," in *Critical Inquiry* 2 (Autumn 1975): 61.

11. William Butler Yeats, *The Poems of W. B. Yeats* (New York: Macmillan, 1983), pp. 259–60.

12. Derrida's discussion is subject to Henry Orlov's criticism of musical semiology that it "runs the risk of replacing its object [by] getting lost in sheer speculation." See Henry Orlov, "Towards a Semiotics of Music," in *The Sign in Music and Literature*, ed. Wendy Steiner (Austin: University of Texas Press, 1981), p. 137.

13. Jacques Derrida, "Ulysses Gramophone: Hear Say Yes in Joyce," in *James Joyce: The Augmented Ninth*, ed. Bernard Benstock (Syracuse, N.Y.: Syracuse University Press, 1988), p. 70.

14. Arthur Symons, *The Symbolist Movement in Literature* (New York: E. P. Dutton, 1919).

15. Zack Bowen, *Musical Allusions in the Works of James Joyce* (Albany: SUNY Press, 1974); and M. J. C. Hodgard and M. P. Worthington, *Song in the Works of James Joyce* (New York: Columbia University Press, 1959).

16. Di Gaetani, *Richard Wagner and the Modern British Novel*, Chapter 5.

17. Richard Ellmann, *James Joyce,* rev. ed. (New York: Oxford University Press, 1982), pp. 73–75.

18. James S. Atherton, *The Books at the Wake: A Study of Literary Allusions in Joyce's Finnegans Wake* (New York: Viking, 1960), p. 48.

19. James Joyce, *A Portrait of the Artist as a Young Man* (New York: Viking, 1964), p. 167.

20. Joyce, *Critical Writings*, p. 75.

21. Samuel Beckett, "Dante . . . Bruno. Vico . . . Joyce," in *Our Exagmination Round*

His Factification For Incamination of Work in Progress (Norfolk: New Directions, 1939), p. 14.

22. Joyce, *A Portrait*, p. 167.

23. S. L. Goldberg, *The Classical Temper: A Study of James Joyce's Ulysses* (London: Chatto and Windus, 1961), pp. 233–34.

24. Joyce, *A Portrait*, p. 215.

25. Joyce, *Critical Writings*, p. 67.

26. Ibid., p. 45.

27. Ibid., p. 67.

28. Hugh Kenner, *Dublin's Joyce* (Boston: Beacon Press, 1956), p. 87.

29. Ellmann, *James Joyce*, p. 299.

30. Karen Lawrence, *The Odyssey of Style in Ulysses* (Princeton: Princeton University Press, 1982), pp. 91–93.

31. Hugh Kenner, *Joyce's Voices* (Berkeley: University of California Press, 1978), pp. 41–49.

32. Morris Beja et al., *James Joyce: The Centennial Symposium* (Urbana: University of Illinois Press, 1986).

33. James Joyce, *Ulysses*, ed. Hans W. Gabler (New York: Vintage, 1986), pp. 226–27; all future references in the text are to this edition.

34. Cheryl Herr, "Nature and Culture in the 'Sirens' Episode of Joyce's *Ulysses*," in *Modern Critical Interpretations of James Joyce's Ulysses*, ed. Harold Bloom (New York: Chelsea House, 1986), p. 134.

35. Ibid., p. 139.

36. Robert M. Adams, *Surface and Symbol: The Consistency of James Joyce's Ulysses* (New York: Oxford University Press, 1962).

37. Frank Kermode, *The Sense of an Ending: Studies in the Theory of Fiction* (New York: Oxford University Press, 1967), p. 113.

38. Nietzsche, *Basic Writings*, pp. 98, 106.

39. Kermode, *The Sense of an Ending*, p. 179.

40. Richard Ellmann, *Ulysses on the Liffey* (New York: Oxford University Press, 1972), pp. 101 ff.

41. Adams, *Surface and Symbol*, p. 254.

42. Ellmann, *James Joyce*, pp. 156–57.

43. Suzanne Langer, *Philosophy in a New Key* (New York: NAL, 1948), pp. 206 ff.

44. David Daiches, *The Novel and the Modern World* (Chicago: University of Chicago Press, 1960), pp. 114–16.

45. Fritz Senn, "Righting Joyce," in *James Joyce: New Perspectives*, ed. Colin McCabe (Bloomington: Indiana University Press, 1982), p. 11.

46. Ibid., p. 14.

47. Ibid., p. 19.

48. Leslie Fiedler, "Bloom on Joyce: or, Jokey for Jacob," in *New Light on Joyce from the Dublin Symposium*, ed. Fritz Senn (Bloomington: Indiana University Press, 1972).

Notes

49. Claude Lévi-Strauss, *The Raw and the Cooked*, trans. J. and D. Weightman (New York: Harper and Row, 1969), p. 26.

50. Northrop Frye, *Fables of Identity* (New York: Harcourt Brace, 1963), p. 264.

Chapter 8. Conclusion

1. Martin Jay, *Adorno* (London: Fontana, 1984), p. 54.
2. Bloch, *Philosophy of Music*, p. xxiii.
3. Schorer, *The World We Imagine*, p. 120.
4. Kermode, *The Sense of an Ending*, p. 179.
5. Ibid., p. 178.
6. Rilke, *Selected Poetry*, p.147.
7. Walter Strauss, *Descent and Return: The Orphic Theme in Modern Literature* (Cambridge: Harvard University Press, 1971), p. 184.
8. Rilke, *Selected Poetry*, p. 231.
9. Yeats, *Collected Poems*, p. 191.
10. T. S. Eliot, *Collected Poems: 1909–1962* (San Diego: Harcourt Brace Jovanovich, 1963).
11. Ortega y Gasset, *Selections from Towards a Philosophy of History*, in *Existentialism from Dostoyevsky to Sartre*, ed. Walter Kaufmann (New York: NAL, 1975), p. 156; see also Alexander Nehamas, *Nietzsche: Life as Literature* (Cambridge: Harvard University Press, 1985), p. 228.

Works Cited

Abrams, M. H. *The Mirror and the Lamp.* New York: W. W. Norton, 1953.
Adams, Robert M. *Strains of Discord: Studies in Literary Openness.* Ithaca: Cornell University Press, 1958.
———. *Surface and Symbol: The Consistency of James Joyce's Ulysses.* New York: Oxford University Press, 1962.
Adorno, Theodor W. *Aesthetic Theory.* Translated by C. Lenhardt. London: Routledge and Kegan Paul, 1984.
———. *Introduction to the Sociology of Music.* Translated by E. B. Ashton. New York: Seabury Press, 1976.
———. *Minima Moralis: Reflections from Damaged Life.* Translated by E. F. N. Sephcott. London: NLB, 1974.
———. *Philosophy of Modern Music.* Translated by Anne Mitchell and Wesley Bloomster. New York: Seabury Press, 1973.
———. *Prisms.* Translated by Samuel and Shierry Weber. Cambridge: MIT Press, 1981.
Allison, David B. "Introduction" to *The New Nietzsche: Contemporary Styles in Interpretation.* New York: Dell, 1977.
Allott, Miriam, editor. *Novelists on the Novel.* New York: Columbia University Press, 1959.
Altieri, Charles. "Ecce Homo: Narcissism, Power, Pathos, and the Status of Autobiographical Representation." In *Why Nietzsche Now?* edited by Daniel O'Hara. Bloomington: Indiana University Press, 1985.
Arac, Jonathan. "Aesthetics, Rhetoric, History: Paul de Man and the American Use of Nietzsche." In *Why Nietzsche Now?* edited by Daniel O'Hara. Bloomington: Indiana University Press, 1985.
Aronson, Alex. *Music and the Novel: A Study in Twentieth Century Fiction.* Totowa, N.J.: Rowman and Littlefield, 1980.
Atherton, James S. *The Books at the Wake: A Study of Literary Allusions in Joyce's Finnegans Wake.* New York: Viking, 1960.
Attali, Jacques. Noise: *The Political Economy of Music.* Translated by Brian Massumi. Minneapolis: University of Minnesota Press, 1985.
Bakhtin, M. M. *Problems of Dostoyevsky's Poetics.* Translated by Caryl Emerson. Minneapolis: University of Minnesota Press, 1984.

Works Cited

Barthes, Roland. "Musica Practica" in *Image/Music/Text*. Translated by Stephen Heath. New York: Hill & Wang, 1977.

———. *S/Z*. Translated by Richard Miller. New York: Hill & Wang, 1974.

Baudelaire, Charles. *The Flowers of Evil*. Selected and edited by M. and J. Matthews. Revised Edition. Norfolk: New Directions, 1963.

Beckett, Samuel. "Dante . . . Bruno. Vico . . . Joyce." In *Our Exagmination Round His Factification For Incamination of Work in Progress*. Norfolk: New Directions, 1939.

———. *Proust*. New York: Grove Press, 1957.

Beethoven, Ludwig van. *Piano Sonatas*. Urtext edition. Berlin: Henle, 1960.

Beja, Morris, et al., editors. *James Joyce: The Centennial Symposium*. Urbana: University of Illinois Press, 1986.

Benjamin, Walter. *Illuminations*. Translated by Harry Zohn. New York: Harcourt Brace Jovanovich, 1968.

Bersani, Leo. "Lawrentian Stillness." In *A Future for Astynanax: Character and Desire in Literature*. Boston: Little Brown, 1976.

———. "Proust and the Art of Incompletion." In *Aspects of Narrative*, edited by J. Hillis Miller. New Haven: Yale University Press, 1977.

Bergsten, Gunilla. *Thomas Mann's Doctor Faustus*. Chicago: University of Chicago Press, 1969.

Blanchot, Maurice. *The Sirens' Song*. Translated by Sacha Rabinovitch. Bloomington: Indiana University Press, 1982.

Bloch, Ernst. *Essays on the Philosophy of Music*. Translated by Peter Palmer. Introduction by David Drew. Cambridge: Cambridge University Press, 1985.

———. *The Utopian Function of Art and Literature: Selected Essays*. Translated by Jack Zipes and Frank Mecklenburg. Cambridge: MIT Press, 1988.

Bloom, Harold. *Wallace Stevens: The Poems of Our Climate*. Ithaca: Cornell University Press, 1977.

Bowen, Zack. *Musical Allusions in the Works of James Joyce*. Albany: SUNY Press, 1974.

Broch, Herman. *Death of Virgil*. Translated by Jean Starr Untermeyer. New York: Pantheon, 1945.

Brown, Calvin S. *Music and Literature: A Comparison of the Arts*. Athens: University of Georgia Press, 1948.

Burke, Kenneth. "Thomas Mann and Andre Gidé." In *Counter-Statements*. Los Altos, Calif.: Hermes, 1953.

Busoni, Ferruccio. *The Essence of Music and Other Essays*. Translated by Rosamond Ley. New York: Dover, 1965.

Camus, Albert. *The Myth of Sisyphus and Other Essays*. Translated by Justin O'Brien. New York: Vintage, 1960.

Carnegy, Patrick. *Faust as Musician: A Study of Thomas Mann's Novel* Doctor Faustus. New York: New Directions, 1973.

Cavell, Stanley. "Music Discomposed." In *Must We Mean What We Say?* Cambridge: Cambridge University Press, 1976.

Conrad, Joseph. *The Nigger of the 'Narcissus.'* Garden City, N.Y.: Doubleday, Page and Co., 1924.

———. *Notes on Life and Letters*. Garden City, N.Y.: Doubleday, Page and Co., 1925.

———. *Youth and Two Other Stories*. Garden City, N.Y.: Doubleday, Page and Co., 1927.

Works Cited

Corngold, Stanley. "Mann as a Reader of Nietzsche." In *The Fate of the Self: German Writers and French Theory.* New York: Columbia University Press, 1986.

Dahlhaus, Carl. *Between Romanticism and Modernism: Four Studies in the Music of the Later Nineteenth Century.* Translated by Mary Whittall. Berkeley: University of California Press, 1980.

———. "Fiktive Zwölftonmusik: Thomas Mann und Theordor W. Adorno." In *Deutsche Akademie für Sprache und Dichtung,* Darmstadt Jarbuch 1, 1982.

———. *Schoenberg and the New Music.* Translated by Derrick Puffett and Alfred Clayton. New York: Cambridge University Press, 1987.

Daiches, David. *The Novel and the Modern World.* Chicago: University of Chicago Press, 1960.

Danto, Arthur C. *Nietzsche as Philosopher.* New York: Macmillan, 1965.

Deleuze, Gilles. "Active and Reactive" and "Nomad Thought." In *The New Nietzsche,* edited by David Allison. New York: Dell, 1977.

———. *Proust and Signs.* Translated by Richard Howard. New York: George Braziller, 1972.

De Man, Paul. *Allegories of Reading.* New Haven: Yale University Press, 1979.

———. *Blindness and Insight.* New Haven: Oxford University Press, 1971.

Derrida, Jacques. *Of Grammatology.* Translated by G. Chakravorty Spivak. Baltimore: Johns Hopkins University Press, 1977.

———. *Spurs: Nietzsche's Styles.* Translated by Barbara Harlow. Chicago: University of Chicago Press, 1979.

———. "*Ulysses* Gramophone: Hear Say Yes in Joyce." In *James Joyce: The Augmented Ninth,* edited by Matthew Broccoli. Syracuse, N.Y.: Syracuse University Press, 1988.

Dews, Peter. "Adorno, Poststructuralism, and the Critique of Identity." In *The Problems of Identity: Adorno and Benjamin,* edited by Andrew Benjamin. London: Routledge and Kegan Paul, 1989.

DiGaetani, John Louis. *Richard Wagner and the Modern British Novel.* Rutherford, N.J.: Fairleigh Dickinson University Press, 1978.

Eagleton, Terry. *The Ideology of the Aesthetic.* Oxford: Basil Blackwell, 1990.

Eliot, Thomas Stearns. *Collected Poems: 1919–1962.* San Diego: Harcourt, Brace, Jovanovitch, 1963.

Ellmann, Richard. *James Joyce.* Revised edition. New York: Oxford University Press, 1982.

———. *Ulysses on the Liffey.* New York: Oxford University Press, 1972.

Fiedelson, Charles. *Symbolism and American Literature.* Chicago: University of Chicago Press, 1953.

Fiedler, Leslie. "Bloom on Joyce: or, Jokey for Jacob." In *New Light on Joyce from the Dublin Symposium,* edited by Fritz Senn. Bloomington: Indiana University Press, 1972.

Flanagan, Thomas. "Yeats, Joyce, and the Matter of Ireland." In *Critical Inquiry* 2:1 (Autumn 1975).

Flaubert, Gustave. *Madame Bovary.* Translated by Paul de Man. Norton Critical Edition. New York: W. W. Norton, 1965.

Flores, Angel, editor. *An Anthology of French Poetry from Nerval to Valery.* Garden City, N.Y.: Doubleday, 1958.

Forster, E. M. *Aspects of the Novel*. New York: Harcourt Brace, 1954.
———. *Howards End*. New York: Knopf, 1921.
———. *A Passage to India*. New York: Harcourt Brace, 1924.
———. *Two Cheers for Democracy*. London: Edward Arnold, 1972.
Foster, John Burt. *Heirs to Dionysus: A Nietzschean Current in Literary Modernism*. Princeton: Princeton University Press, 1981.
Foucault, Michael. *Language/Countermemory/Practice*. Translated by Donald F. Bouchard and Sherry Simon. Ithaca: Cornell University Press, 1977.
Frye, Northrop. "Quest and Cycle in *Finnegans Wake*." In *Fables of Identity*. New York: Harcourt Brace, 1963.
Genette, Gerard. "Time and Narrative in *À la recherche du temps perdu*." In *Marcel Proust: Modern Critical Views*, edited by Harold Bloom. New York: Chelsea House, 1987.
Gide, André. *The Counterfeiters*. Translated by Dorothy Bussy. New York: Knopf, 1951.
Gilbert, Stuart. *James Joyce's Ulysses*. New York: Vintage, 1952.
Goethe, J. W. *Faust*. Translated by Louis MacNiece. New York: Oxford University Press, 1960.
Goldberg, S. L. *The Classical Temper: A Study of James Joyce's Ulysses*. London: Chatto and Windus, 1961.
Guerard, Albert. *André Gide*. Cambridge: Harvard University Press, 1951.
Hartman, Geoffrey. *Criticism in the Wilderness: The Study of Literature Today*. New Haven: Yale University Press, 1980.
Hassan, Ihab. *The Dismemberment of Orpheus: Towards a Post-modern Literature*. New York: Oxford University Press, 1971.
Heller, Erich. *The Artist's Journey into the Interior*. New York: Vintage, 1968.
———. *The Disinherited Mind*. Cleveland: World Publishing, 1959.
———. *In the Age of Prose*. New York: Cambridge University Press, 1984.
———. *The Ironic German*. Boston: Little Brown, 1958.
Herr, Cheryl. "Nature and Culture in the 'Sirens' Episode of Joyce's *Ulysses*." In *James Joyce's Ulysses: Modern Critical Interpretations*, edited by Harold Bloom. New York: Chelsea House, 1986.
Hesse, Herman. *The Glass Bead Game*. Translated by Richard and Clara Winston. New York: Holt, Rinehart, Winston, 1969.
———. *Steppenwolf*. Translated by Basil Creighton. New York: Holt, Rinehart, Winston, 1961.
Higgins, Kathleen. *Nietzsche's Zarathustra*. Philadelphia: Temple University Press, 1987.
Hodgard, M. J. C., and M. P. Worthington. *Song in the Works of James Joyce*. New York: Columbia University Press, 1959.
Honsa, William M. Jr. "Parody and Narrator in Thomas Mann's *Doctor Faustus*." In *Thomas Mann: Modern Critical Views*. Edited by Harold Bloom. New York: Chelsea House, 1986.
Huxley, Aldous. *Point Counter Point*. Garden City, N.Y.: Doubleday, Doran, 1928.
Jameson, Frederic. "Introduction" to Jacques Attali's *Noise*. Minneapolis: University of Minnesota Press, 1985.
———. *The Theory of Ideology* Vol. II: *The Syntax of History*. Minneapolis: University of Minnesota Press, 1988.

Works Cited

Jay, Martin. *Adorno*. London: Fontana, 1984.
Joyce, James. *The Critical Writings of James Joyce*. Edited by Ellsworth Mason and Richard Ellmann. New York: Viking, 1959.
———. *A Portrait of the Artist as a Young Man*. New York: Viking, 1964.
———. *Ulysses*. Edited by Hans W. Gabler. New York: Vintage, 1986.
Kafka, Franz. *The Penal Colony: Stories and Short Pieces*. Translated by Willa and Edwin Muir. New York: Schocken, 1948.
Kahler, Erick. "*Doctor Faustus*: The Devil Secularized" in *The Orbit of Thomas Mann*. Princeton: Princeton University Press, 1969.
Kandinsky, Wassily. *Arnold Schoenberg–Wassily Kandinsky: Letters, Pictures and Documents*. Translated by John C. Crawford. London: Faber and Faber, 1984.
Karl, Frederick. *Modern and Modernism*. New York: Atheneum, 1988.
Kaufmann, Walter. *Nietzsche: Philosopher Psychologist Antichrist*. New York: Meridian Books, 1956.
Kenner, Hugh. *Dublin's Joyce*. Boston: Beacon Press, 1956.
———. *Joyce's Voices*. Berkeley: University of California Press, 1978.
Kerman, Joseph. *Contemplating Music: Challenges to Musicology*. Cambridge: Harvard University Press, 1985.
———. *Opera as Drama*. Revised Edition. Berkeley: University of California Press, 1988.
Kermode, Frank. *The Sense of an Ending: Studies in the Theory of Fiction*. New York: Oxford University Press, 1967.
Klossowski, Pierre. "Nietzsche's Experience of the Eternal Return." In *The New Nietzsche,* edited by David Allison. New York: Dell, 1977.
Kofman, Sarah. "Metaphor, Symbol, Metamorphosis." In *The New Nietzsche*. Edited by David Allison. New York: Dell, 1977.
Kreneck, Ernst. *Music Here and Now*. Translated by B. Fles. New York: W. W. Norton, 1939.
Kroker, Arthur, and David Cook. *The Postmodern Scene: Excremental Culture and Hyper-Aesthetics*. New York: St. Martin's, 1988.
Langbaum, Robert. *The Mysteries of Identity: A Theme in Modern Literature*. New York: Oxford University Press, 1977.
Langer, Suzanne. *Philosophy in a New Key*. New York: NAL, 1948.
Lawrence, D. H. *Aaron's Rod*. 1922; New York: Penguin, 1976.
———. *Apocalypse*. 1931; New York: Penguin, 1976.
———. *The Man Who Died*. 1928. Reprint. New York: Vintage, 1953.
———. *Phoenix II*. New York: Penguin, 1978.
———. *Women in Love*. 1920; Reprint. New York: Penguin, 1982.
Lawrence, Karen. *The Odyssey of Style in Ulysses*. Princeton: Princeton University Press, 1982.
Lehmann, A. G. *The Symbolist Aesthetic in France 1885–95*. Oxford: Basil Blackwell, 1968.
Lévesque, Claude. "Dissonance." In *Études Francaises,* October 17 1981 (3–4).
———. "Language to the Limit." In *Nietzsche and the Rhetoric of Nihilism*. Edited by Tom Darby, Bela Egyed, and Ben Jones. Ottawa: Carleton University Press, 1989.
Levin, Gerald. "The Musical Style of *The Waves*." In *Journal of Narrative Technique* 13:3 (Fall 1983).

Lévi-Strauss, Claude. *The Raw and the Cooked*. Translated by J. and D. Weightman. New York: Harper and Row, 1969.

Lyotard, Jean-François. "Several Silences." In *Driftworks*. Translated by Roger McKeon. New York: Columbia University Press, 1984.

Madou, Jean-Pol. "Langue, mythe, musique: Rousseau, Nietzsche, Mallarmé, Lévi-Strauss." In *Littérature et Musique,* edited by Raphael Celis. Bruxelles: Facultés universitaires Saint Louis, 1982.

Mallarmé, Stéphane. "Music and Literature." Translated by B. Cook. In *Modern Continental Literary Criticism.* Edited by O. B. Hardison. New York: Appleton Century Crofts, 1962.

———. *Selected Poetry and Prose.* Edited by Mary Ann Caws. Norfolk: New Directions, 1982.

Mann, Thomas. *Buddenbrooks.* Translated by H. T. Lowe-Porter. New York: Vintage, 1964.

———. *Death in Venice and Seven Other Stories.* New York: Random House, 1936.

———. *Doctor Faustus.* Translated by H. T. Lowe-Porter. New York: Modern Library, 1948.

———. *Essays of Three Decades.* Translated by H. T. Lowe-Porter. New York: Knopf, 1965.

———. *Letters.* Translated by Richard and Clara Winston. New York: Knopf, 1971.

———. *The Magic Mountain.* Translated by H. T. Lowe-Porter. New York: Modern Library, 1952.

———. *Past Masters.* Translated by H. T. Lowe-Porter. New York: Knopf, 1933.

———. *Pro and Contra Wagner.* Translated by Allan Blunden. Chicago: University of Chicago Press, 1985.

———. *Stories of Three Decades.* Translated by H. T. Lowe-Porter. New York: Knopf, 1936.

———. *The Story of a Novel.* Translated by H. T. Lowe-Porter. New York: Knopf, 1961.

Mellers, Wilfrid. *Caliban Reborn: Renewal in Twentieth Century Music.* New York: Harper and Row, 1967.

Meltzer, Françoise. *Salome and the Dance of Writing.* Chicago: University of Chicago Press, 1987.

Melnick, Daniel. "Dissonant *Ulysses*: A Study of How to Read Joyce." *Twentieth Century Literature* 26:1 (Spring 1980).

———. "Fullness of Dissonance." In *Modern Fiction Studies* 25:2 (Summer 1979).

———. "Proust, Music, and the Reader." In *Modern Language Quarterly* 41:2 (June, 1980).

Meyer, Leonard B. *Music, the Arts, and Ideas.* Chicago: University of Chicago Press, 1967.

Morgan, Robert P. "Secret Languages: The Roots of Musical Modernism." In *Modernism: Challenges and Perspectives,* edited by M. Chefdor, K. Quinones, and A. Wachtel. Urbana: University of Illinois Press, 1986.

Nattiez, Jean-Jacques. *Proust as Musician.* Translated by Derrick Puffett. New York: Cambridge University Press, 1989.

Nehamas, Alexander. "Nietzsche in *The Magic Mountain*," In *Modern Critical Interpretations: Thomas Mann's The Magic Mountain*, edited by Harold Bloom. New York: Chelsea House, 1986.

———. *Nietzsche: Life as Literature.* Cambridge: Harvard University Press, 1985.

Nietzsche, Friedrich. *Basic Writings of Friederich Nietzsche.* Translated by Walter Kaufmann. New York: Modern Library, 1968.

———. *Portable Nietzsche.* Translated by Walter Kaufmann. New York: Viking/Penguin, 1954.
Norris, Christopher. *Deconstructionism: Theory and Practice.* New York: Methuen, 1982.
———. "Utopian Deconstruction: Ernst Bloch, Paul de Man and the Politics of Music." In *Paragraph* 88, 11:1 (March 1988).
Orlov, Henry. "Towards a Semiotics of Music." In *The Sign in Music and Literature,* edited by Wendy Steiner. Austin: University of Texas Press, 1981.
Ortega y Gasset, José. *Selection from Towards a Philosophy of History.* In *Existentialism from Dostoyevsky to Sartre,* edited by Walter Kaufmann. New York: NAL, 1975.
Osborne, Peter. "Adorno and the Metaphysics of Modernism: The Problem of 'Postmodern' Art." In *The Problems of Modernity: Adorno and Benjamin,* edited by Andrew Benjamin. London: Routledge and Kegan Paul, 1989.
Painter, George. *Proust: The Later Years.* Boston: Little Brown, 1965.
Pater, Walter. *Studies in the Renaissance.* Cleveland: World, 1961.
Piroué, Georges. *Proust et la musique du devenir.* Paris: Editions Denoel, 1960.
Pound, Ezra. "M. James Joyce et Pécuchet." In *Polite Essays.* New York: Books for Libraries Press, 1937.
Proust, Marcel. *À la recherche du temps perdu.* Pléiade edition. Edited by Clarac and Ferre. Bruges: Gallimard, 1954.
———. *Remembrance of Things Past.* Translated by C. K. Scott Moncrieff and Terence Kilmartin. New York: Random House, 1981.
Rilke, Rainer Maria. *Selected Poetry of Rainer Maria Rilke.* Translated by Stephen Mitchell. New York: Vintage, 1984.
Rodman, Selden. *The Heart of Beethoven.* New York: Shorewood, 1962.
Rosen, Charles. *Arnold Schoenberg.* New York: Viking, 1975.
Rousseau, Jean-Jacques. *Essay on the Origin of Languages.* Translated by John H. Moran and Alexander Gode. Chicago: University of Chicago Press, 1966.
———. *The Reveries of a Solitary.* Translated by J. B. Fletcher. New York: Burt Franklin, 1971.
Sartre, Jean Paul. *What Is Literature? (Situations II).* Translated by Bernard Frechtman. New York: Harper and Row, 1965.
Scaff, Susan von Rohr. "Unending Apocalypse: The Crisis in Musical Narrative in Mann's *Doktor Faustus.*" In *Germanic Review* 65:1 (Winter 1990).
Scher, Steven Paul. "Literature and Music." In *Interrelations of Literature,* edited by Jean-Pierre Barricelli and Joseph Gibaldi. New York: MLA, 1982.
Schoenberg, Arnold. *Moses und Aron.* New York: Schott and Co., 1952.
———. *Second String Quartet, Opus 10.* New York: Schirmer, 1939.
——— *Style and Idea.* Translated by Leonard Stein. New York: Philosophical Library, 1950.
Schoolfield, George. *The Figure of the Musician in German Literature.* Chapel Hill: University of North Carolina Press, 1956.
Schopenhauer, Arthur. *Schopenhauer: Selections.* Edited and translated by D. H. Parker. New York: Scribner's, 1956.
Schorer, Mark. *The World We Imagine: Selected Essays.* New York: Farrar, Straus and Giroux, 1968.
Schorske, Carl. *Fin-de-Siècle Vienna: Politics and Culture.* New York: Knopf, 1980.
Schrade, Leo. *Beethoven in France: The Growth of an Idea.* New Haven: Yale University Press, 1942.

———. *Tragedy in the Art of Music.* Cambridge: Harvard University Press, 1964.
Schumann, Robert. "Davidsbündlerblatter." In *Source Readings in Music History: The Romantic Era,* edited by Oliver Strunk. New York: W. W. Norton, 1965.
Senn, Fritz. *Joyce's Dislocutions: Essays on Reading as Translation.* Edited by John Paul Riquelme. Baltimore: Johns Hopkins University Press, 1984.
———. "Righting Joyce." In *James Joyce: New Perspectives,* edited by Colin McCabe. Bloomington: Indiana University Press, 1982.
Shattuck, Roger. "The Devil's Dance: Stravinsky's Corporeal Imagination." In *The Innocent Eye.* New York: Farrar Strauss Giroux, 1984.
Shepherd, John, et al. *Whose Music? A Sociology of Musical Languages.* New Brunswick, N.J.: Transaction Books, 1977.
Solomon, Maynard. *Beethoven.* New York: Schirmer, 1977.
Steiner, George. *Language and Silence.* London: Faber and Faber, 1967.
Strauss, Walter. *Descent and Return: The Orphic Theme in Modern Literature.* Cambridge: Harvard University Press, 1971.
Stravinsky, Igor. *Poetics of Music.* New York: Vintage, 1959.
Sullivan, J. W. N. *Beethoven: His Spiritual Development.* New York: Vintage, 1960.
Symons, Arthur. The *Symbolist Movement in Literature*. New York: E. P. Dutton, 1919.
Toynbee, Philip. "A Study of James Joyce's *Ulysses.*" In *James Joyce: Two Decades of Criticism,* edited by Seon Givens. New York: Vanguard, 1948.
Turnell, Martin. *Baudelaire: A Study of His Poetry.* London: Hamish Hamilton, 1953.
Wagner, Richard. "The Art Work of the Future." In *Source Readings in Music History: The Romantic Era.* New York: W. W. Norton, 1965.
Webern, Anton. *The Path to the New Music.* New York: Presser, 1963.
Weinstein, Philip. *The Semantics of Desire: Changing Modes of Identity from Dickens to Joyce.* Princeton: Princeton University Press, 1984.
Welleck, René, and Austin Warren. *Theory of Literature.* New York: Harcourt Brace and World, 1956.
Wilde, Alan. *Art and Order: A Study of E. M. Forster.* New York: New York University Press, 1964.
———. *Horizons of Assent: Modernism, Postmodernism, and the Ironic Imagination.* Philadelphia: University of Pennsylvania Press, 1987.
Wilson, Edmund. *Axel's Castle.* New York: Scribner's, 1959.
Winn, James Anderson. *Unsuspected Eloquence.* New Haven: Yale University Press, 1981.
Woolf, Virginia. *Mrs. Dalloway.* New York: Harcourt, Brace, 1925.
———. *The Waves.* New York: Harcourt, Brace, 1931.
Yeats, W. B. *Autobiographies.* New York: Collier, 1965.
———. *The Poems of W. B. Yeats.* Edited by Richard Finneran. New York: Macmillan, 1983.

Index

Adams, Robert M., 117, 119, 132
Adorno, Theodor W., 22–23, 25–27, 43, 45, 55–57, 77, 80, 82–83, 100, 108, 126–27, 131; and the definition of dissonance, 9–11
Allison, David, 46
Altieri, Charles, 51
Arac, Jonathan, 48
Arnold, Matthew, 33
Aronson, Alex, 12
Attali, Jacques, 26, 57

Bakhtin, Mikhail, 28
Barthes, Roland, 3, 27–28, 43, 45, 131
Baudelaire, Charles, 12, 33–35, 41, 81
Beckett, Samuel, 62–63, 74, 108
Beethoven, Ludwig van, 16, 18, 21–28, 32, 34, 43, 45, 52, 56, 134; Piano Sonata #29, opus 106 (Hammerklavier), 22–23, 27; Piano Sonata #32, opus 111, 23, 26, 96; Quartet #14, opus 131, 22; Symphony #5, 103; Symphony #9, 21, 26, 94
Beja, Morris, 115
Benjamin, Walter, 69, 76
Bergson, Henri, 65
Bergsten, Gunilla, 83
Berlioz, Hector, 21, 33, 36
Bersani, Leo, 77, 104
Blake, William, 13
Blanchot, Maurice, 11, 33–35, 54–55, 108, 126–27

Bloch, Ernst, 9–11, 23–24, 43, 45, 77
Bloom, Harold, 48
Bowen, Zack, 107
Brahms, Johannes, 56
Broch, Hermann, 60
Brontë, Emily, 13
Brown, Calvin, 12
Busoni, Ferrico, 22

Cage, John, 57
Camus, Albert, 59
Carlyle, Thomas, 13
Carnegy, Patrick, 83
Cavell, Stanley, 56
Chopin, Frederic, 33
Coleridge, Samuel Taylor, 17
Conrad, Joseph, 4, 8, 13, 30–32, 36, 39–40, 53, 90, 103, 128, 132–33; *Heart of Darkness*, 5–7; "Henry James: An Appreciation," 10; Preface to *The Nigger of the 'Narcissus'*, 6
Cook, David, 57
Corngold, Stanley, 84–85

Dahlhaus, Carl, 12, 15, 51, 56–57, 83
Daiches, David, 121
Danto, Arthur, 49
Debussy, Claude, 14, 56, 81, 93
Deleuze, Gilles, 46, 64, 66
De Man, Paul, 19, 47–48, 66
Derrida, Jacques, 19, 46–47, 84, 106, 131
DiGaetani, John Louis, 41, 107

Dostoyevsky, Fyodor, 28
Dryden, John, 13
Dujardin, Eduard, 38, 41, 106

Eagleton, Terry, 26
Eliot, T. S., 4, 12, 69, 132
Ellmann, Richard, 107, 114, 117–18

Faulkner, William, 80
Fiedler, Leslie, 124
Flanagan, Thomas, 105
Flaubert, Gustave, 35–37
Forster, E. M., 21, 23, 39, 103–4; *Howards End*, 25, 103; *A Passage to India*, 103
Foster, John Burt, 11
Foucault, Michel, 51
Franck, Cesar, 72
Frank, Joseph, 132
Frye, Northrop, 125

Gennette, Gerard, 65, 70
George, Stephan, 55
Gide, André, 8, 61
Goethe, Johann Wolfgang, 16, 88, 93
Goldberg, S. L., 110
Guerard, Albert, 61

Handel, George Friedrich, 13
Hartman, Geoffrey, 3
Hassan, Ihab, 12, 14
Heine, Heinrich, 21
Heller, Erich, 15, 49, 92, 94–95, 97
Herr, Cheryl, 116
Hesse, Hermann, 61
Higgins, Kathleen, 51–52
Hodgard, M. J. C., 107
Huxley, Aldous, 21, 25

Ibsen, Henrik, 41, 107, 111

Jameson, Fredric, 26
Jay, Martin, 126
Joyce, James, 4, 8, 11, 15, 37, 39–41, 58, 61, 83, 90, 100, 101–25; *Chamber Music*, 107–8; *Finnegans Wake*, 108, 125; *A Portrait of the Artist as a Young Man*, 53, 108–13; *Ulysses*, 101–2, 105–7, 112–25, 129–30, 134

Kafka, Franz, 35, 59–60
Kandinsky, Wassily, 14
Karl, Frederick, 14
Kaufmann, Walter, 51
Keats, John, 17–18
Kenner, Hugh, 113, 115
Kerman, Joseph, 24, 42
Kermode, Frank, 95, 117, 132
Klossowski, Pierre, 52
Kroker, Arthur, 57

Langbaum, Robert, 104
Langer, Suzanne, 132, 146
Lawrence, D. H., 4, 21, 39, 44, 90, 104–5; *Aaron's Rod*, 25, 52; *Apocalypse*, 52–53; *The Man Who Died*, 54–55; *Women in Love*, 104, 128–29
Lawrence, Karen, 114
Lehmann, A. G., 31
Lévesque, Claude, 11, 52, 55
Levin, Gerald, 103
Lévi-Strauss, Claude, 124
Liszt, Franz, 33, 36–37
Lyotard, Jean-François, 57–58

Madou, Jean-Paul, 38
Mahler, Gustav, 14, 56, 80–81, 93
Mallarmé, Stéphane, 30, 34, 37–39, 42, 106; as part of the Symbolist Movement, 14, 31, 41, 63–64, 69, 75, 84, 107–8, 110, 112
Mann, Thomas, 4, 8, 11, 21–23, 29–30, 40–41, 44–45, 58, 60–61, 79–100, 105, 111, 116, 123, 131–4; *Buddenbrooks*, 31–32, 79; *Death in Venice*, 80, 85–87; *Doctor Faustus*, 27, 79–85, 90–100, 102, 127–28, 131, 134; *The Magic Mountain*, 80, 85, 87–91
Mellors, Wilfred, 24
Meltzer, Françoise, 13, 38–39
Morgan, Robert, 14
Mozart, Wolfgang Amadeus, 61

Index

Nattiez, Jean-Jacques, 64, 70, 74
Nehamas, Alexander, 51, 144, 147
Nietzsche, Friedrich, 5, 11–12, 29–30, 34, 42–43, 44–56, 61–62, 65–66, 74, 77–78, 84–85, 89, 92–93, 97, 100, 105–7, 111–12, 117, 124–25, 127, 131, 133–34; *The Birth of Tragedy*, 11, 44–45, 49–52; *Ecce Homo*, 11, 49, 51; *The Gay Science*, 45–46; *Geneology of Morals*, 52; *Thus Spoke Zarathustra*, 49, 54; *Twilight of the Idols*, 16–17; *The Wagner Case*, 42, 44
Norris, Chris, 10, 20

Orlov, Henry, 145
Ortega y Gasset, José, 134
Osborne, Peter, 10

Pater, Walter, 3, 6, 8, 10, 30, 39–40, 103, 108
Piroué, Georges, 62–64, 74
Pound, Ezra, 12, 108
Proust, Marcel, 4, 11, 21–22, 31, 37–38, 44, 58, 60–79, 84, 90 111, 123, 127, 132, 134; and Vinteuil, 60–62, 66–73

Quixote, 126–27, 133

Rilke, Rainer Maria, 4, 48, 72–73, 133
Rosen, Charles, 25, 55–57
Rousseau, Jean-Jacques, 12, 16, 18–21, 48, 134
Ruskin, John, 65

Sartre, Jean Paul, 132
Schaff, Susan, 94
Scher, S. P., 41, 74
Schoenberg, Arnold, 14, 55–58, 80, 82–84, 92–93, 126

Schopenhauer, Arnold, 29–33, 42, 61, 64, 66, 69, 75, 84, 96
Schorer, Mark, 5, 129
Schorske, Carl, 14
Schrade, Leo, 21, 23
Schubert, Franz, 18, 32, 89
Schumann, Robert, 33
Senn, Fritz, 124
Shakespeare, William, 13, 108, 119, 122
Shepard, John, 57
Solomon, Maynard, 24
Steiner, George, 5, 11, 60
Sterne, Lawrence, 13
Strauss, Walter, 133
Stravinsky, Igor, 80–83, 93
Swift, Jonathan, 13
Symons, Arthur, 39, 106, 108

Tovey, Donald Francis, 27, 45

Verlaine, Paul, 38, 108

Wagner, Richard, 11, 14, 30, 33, 37, 40–45, 50, 61, 64, 74, 80, 106–7, 111–12; "The Artwork of the Future," 42; *Parsifal*, 41, 70, 111; *The Ring*, 42, 70; *Tristan und Isolde*, 41, 68–70
Webern, Anton, 56
Weinstein, Philip, 11, 104
Welleck, René, 5
Wilde, Alan, 103
Wilde, Oscar, 40
Wilson, Edmund, 62
Winn, James, 57
Woolf, Virginia, 4, 8, 39, 103–4
Worthington, M. P., 107

Yeats, William Butler, 12, 15, 39–40, 105, 132